illustration Coloring Book

Homepage QR Code

flowmusic.kr

© Flow Music

Unauthorized reproduction and reproduction of this book are prohibited.

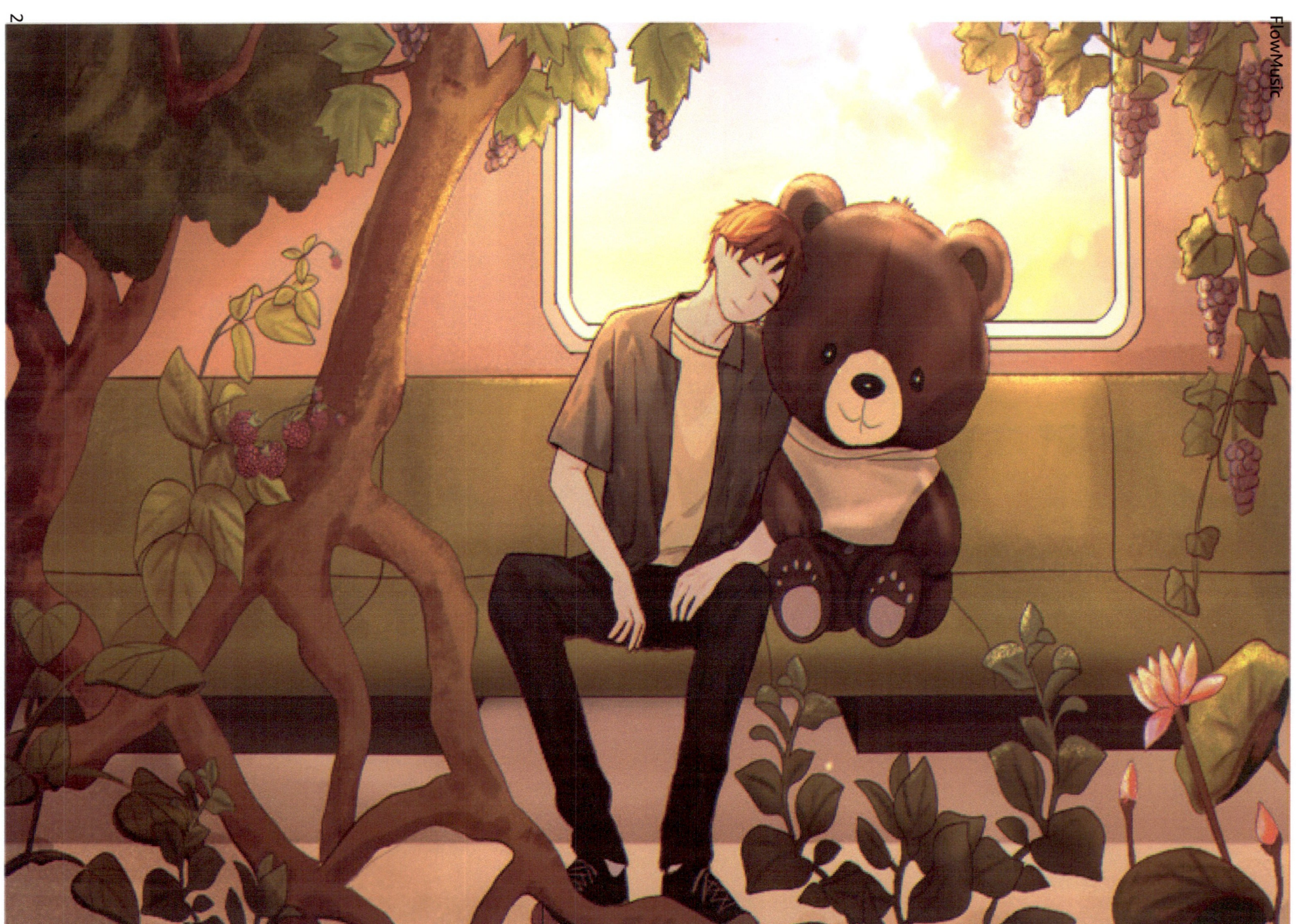

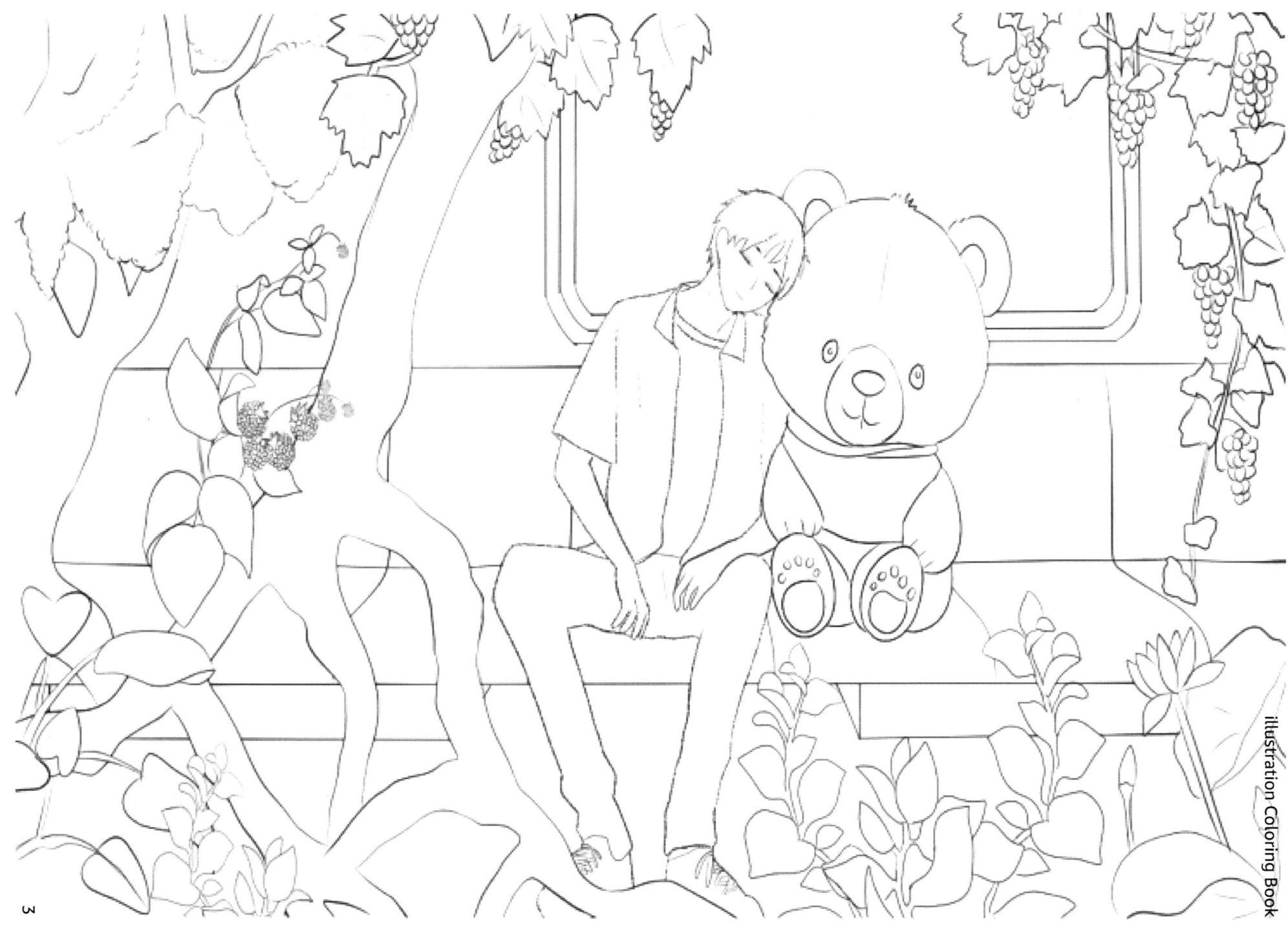

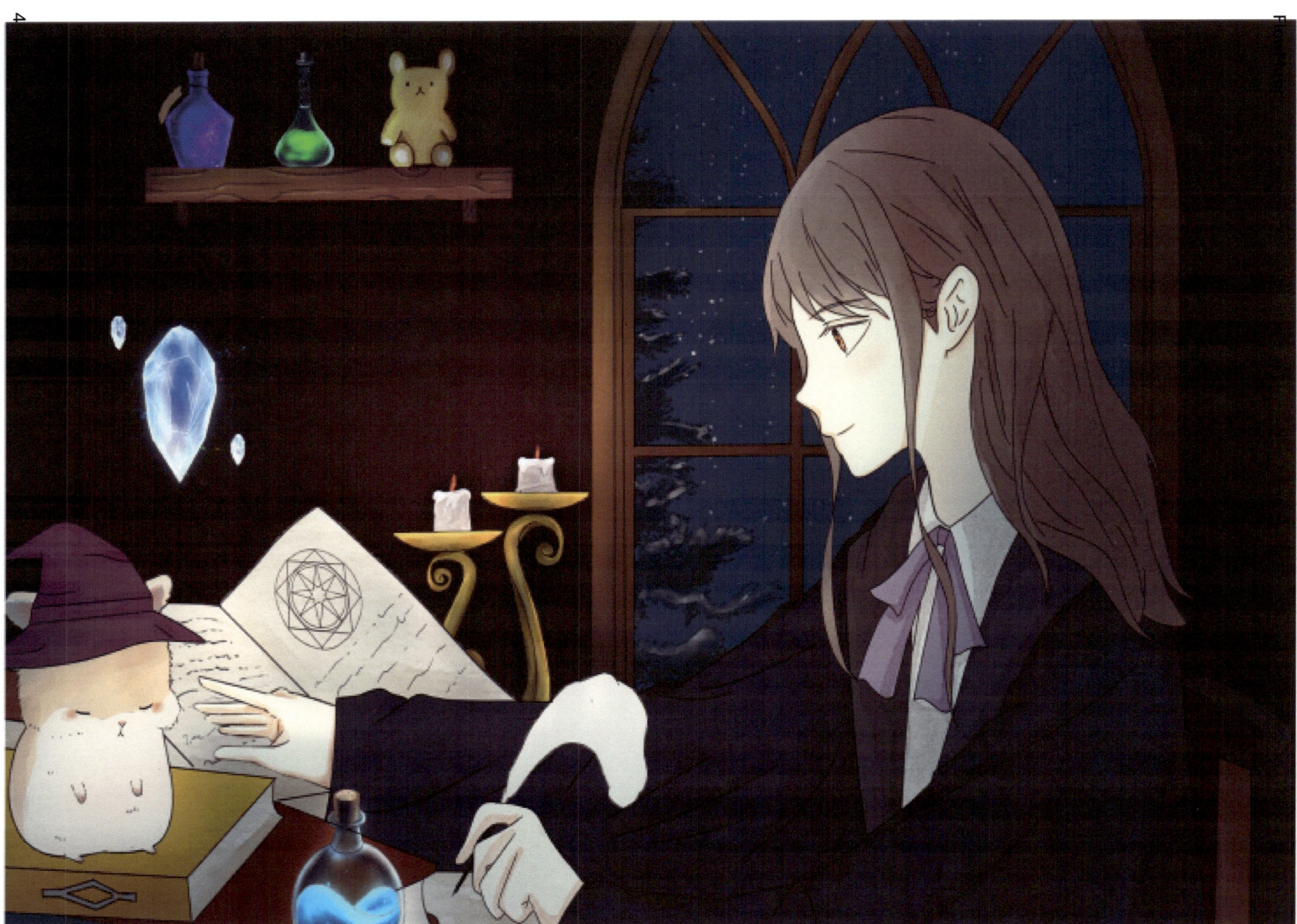

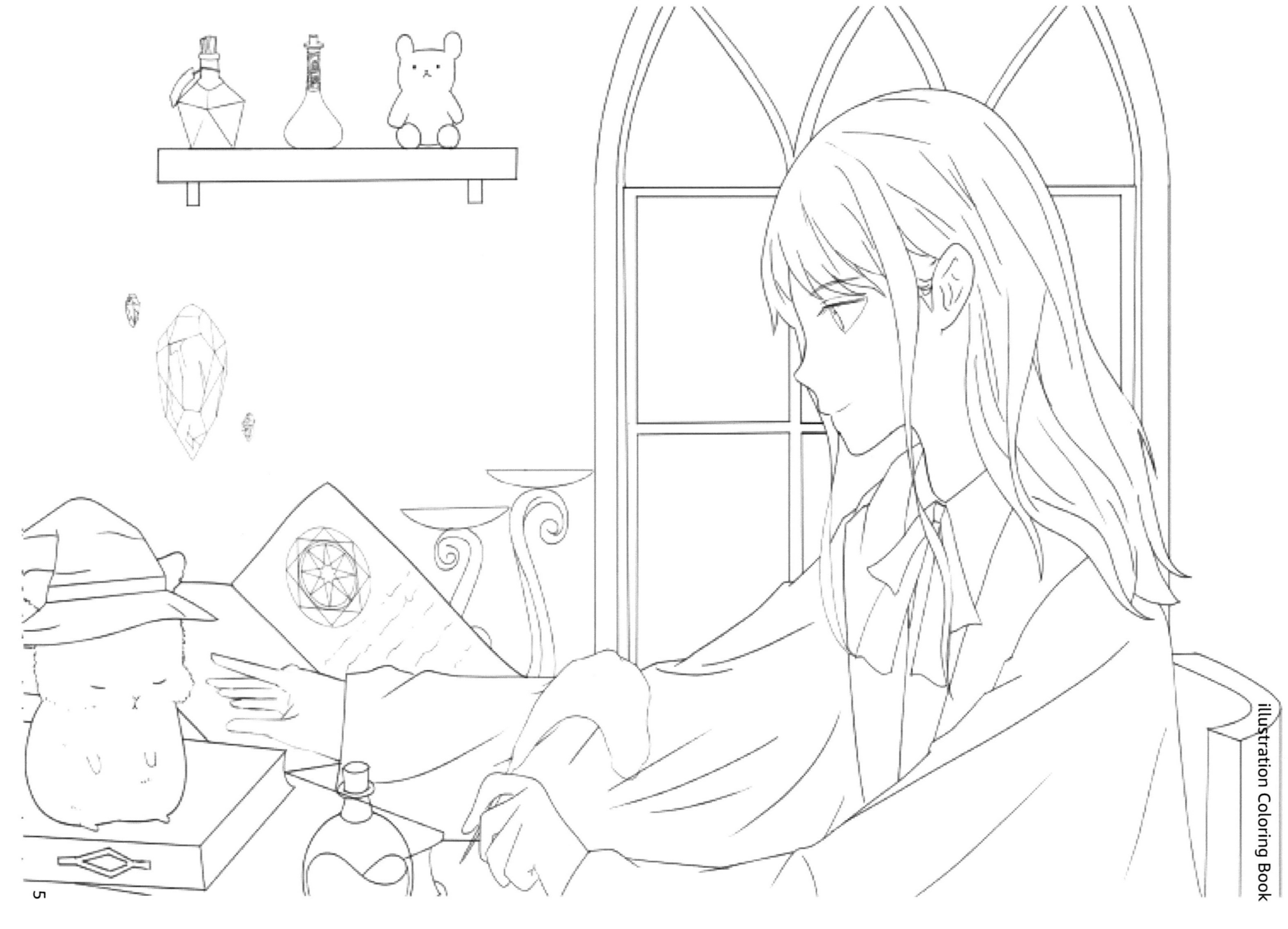

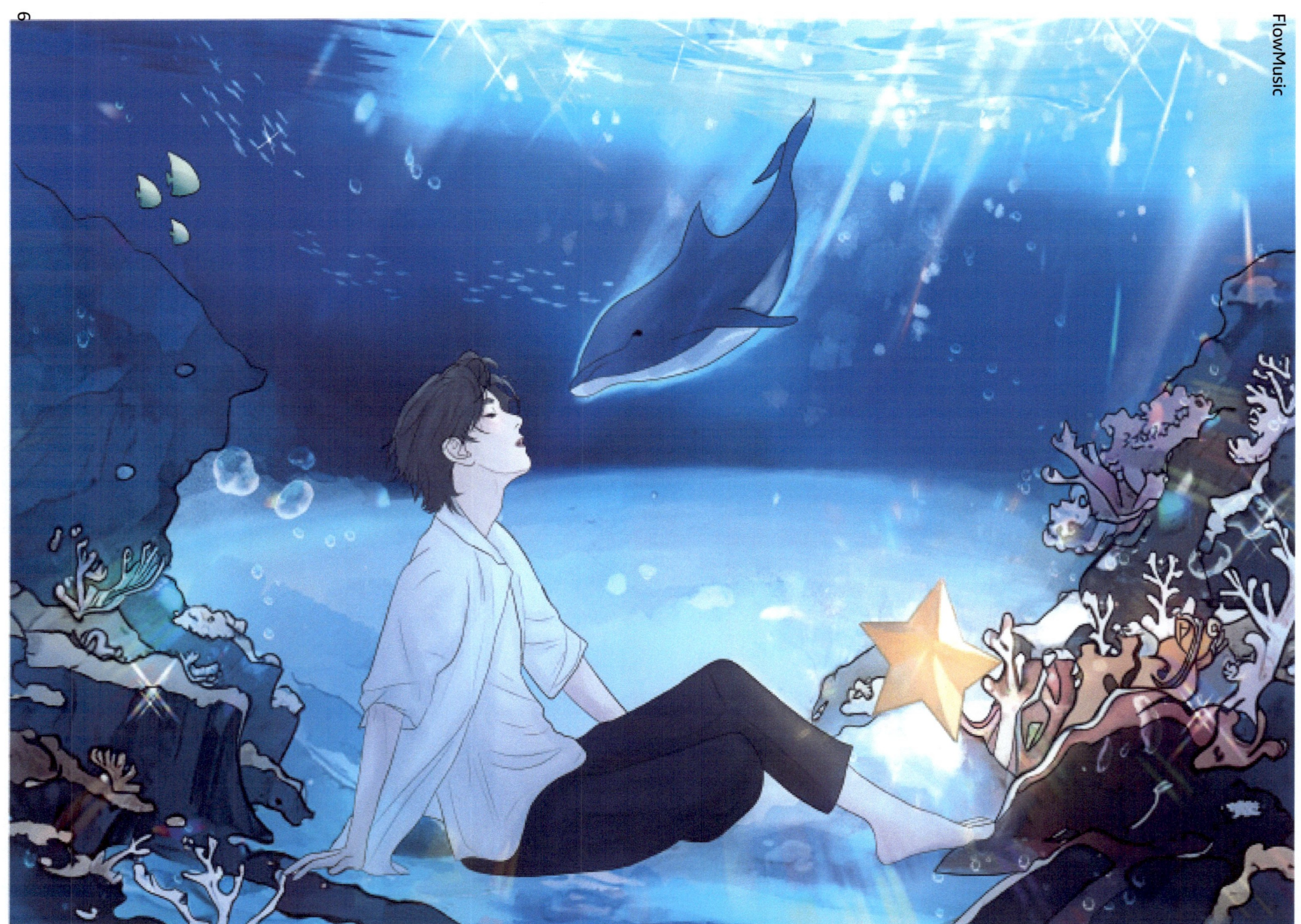

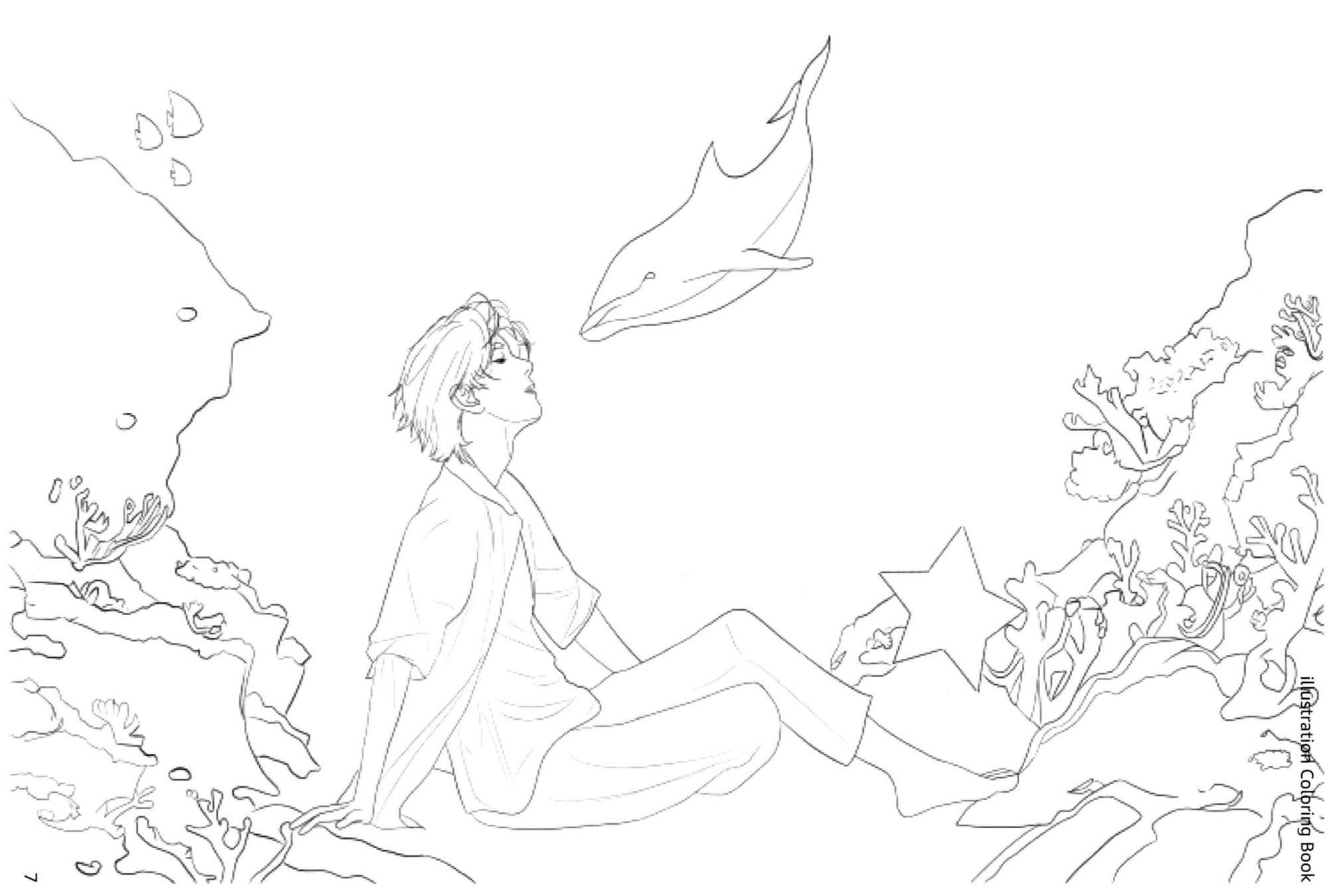

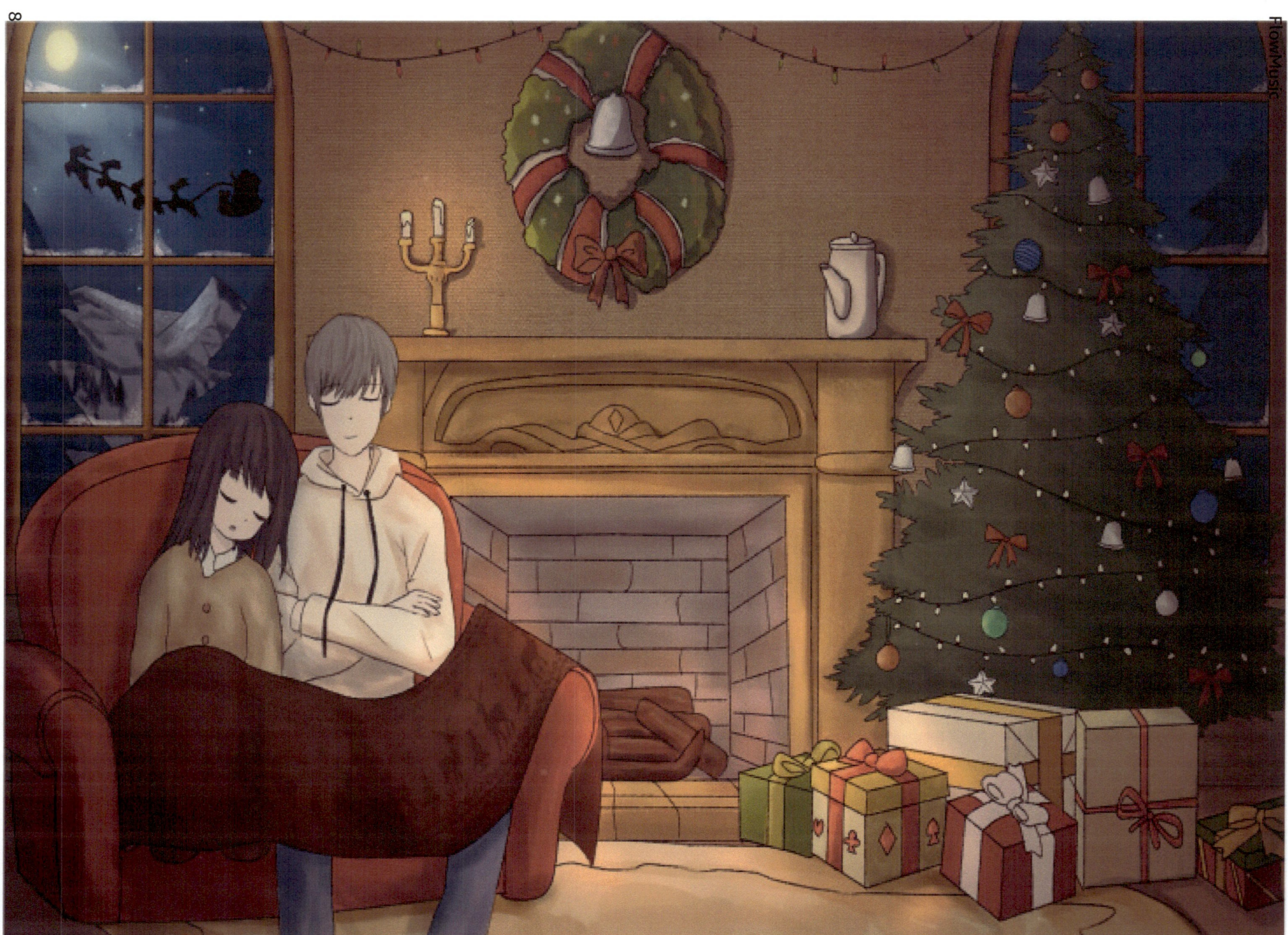

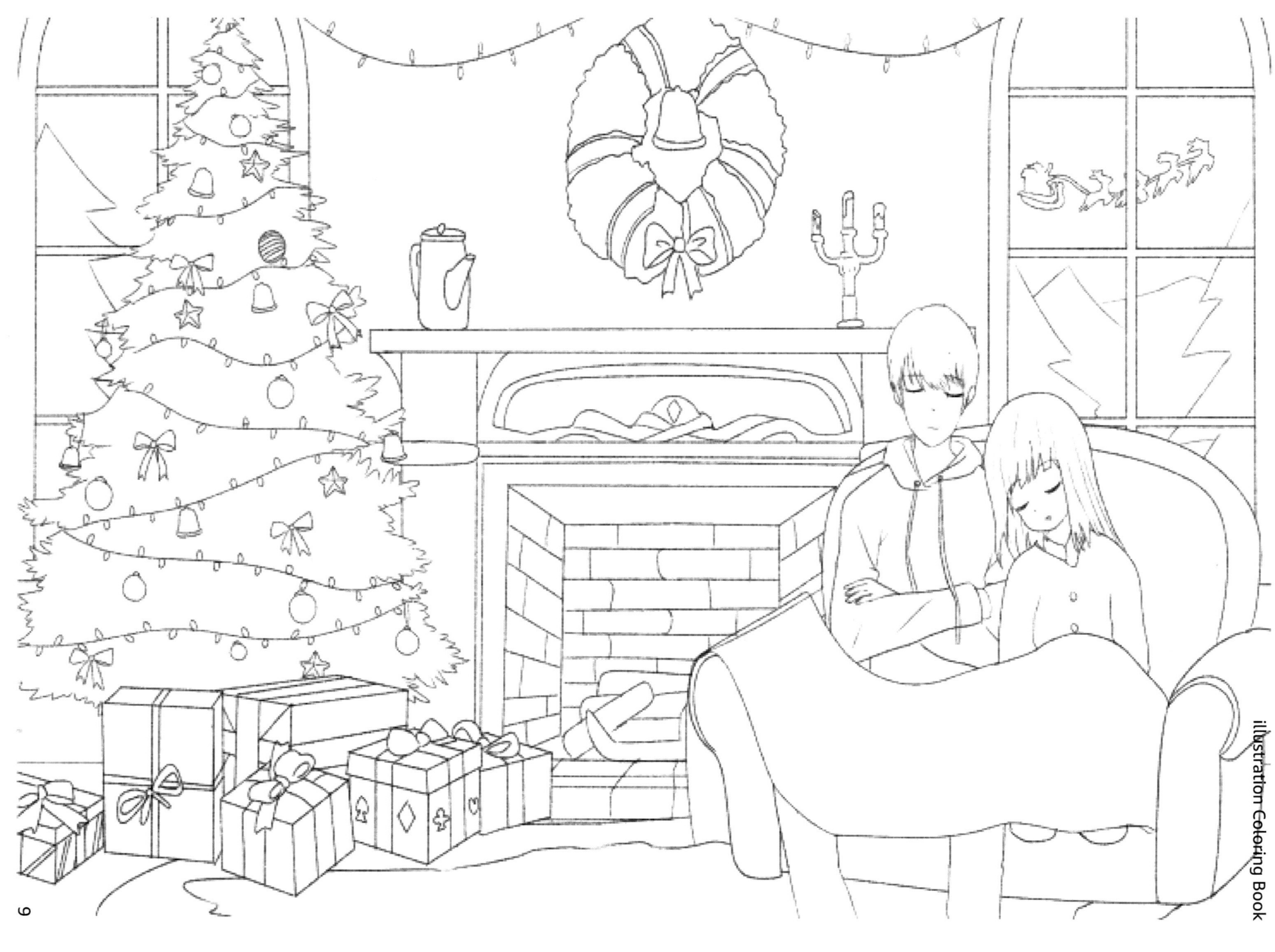

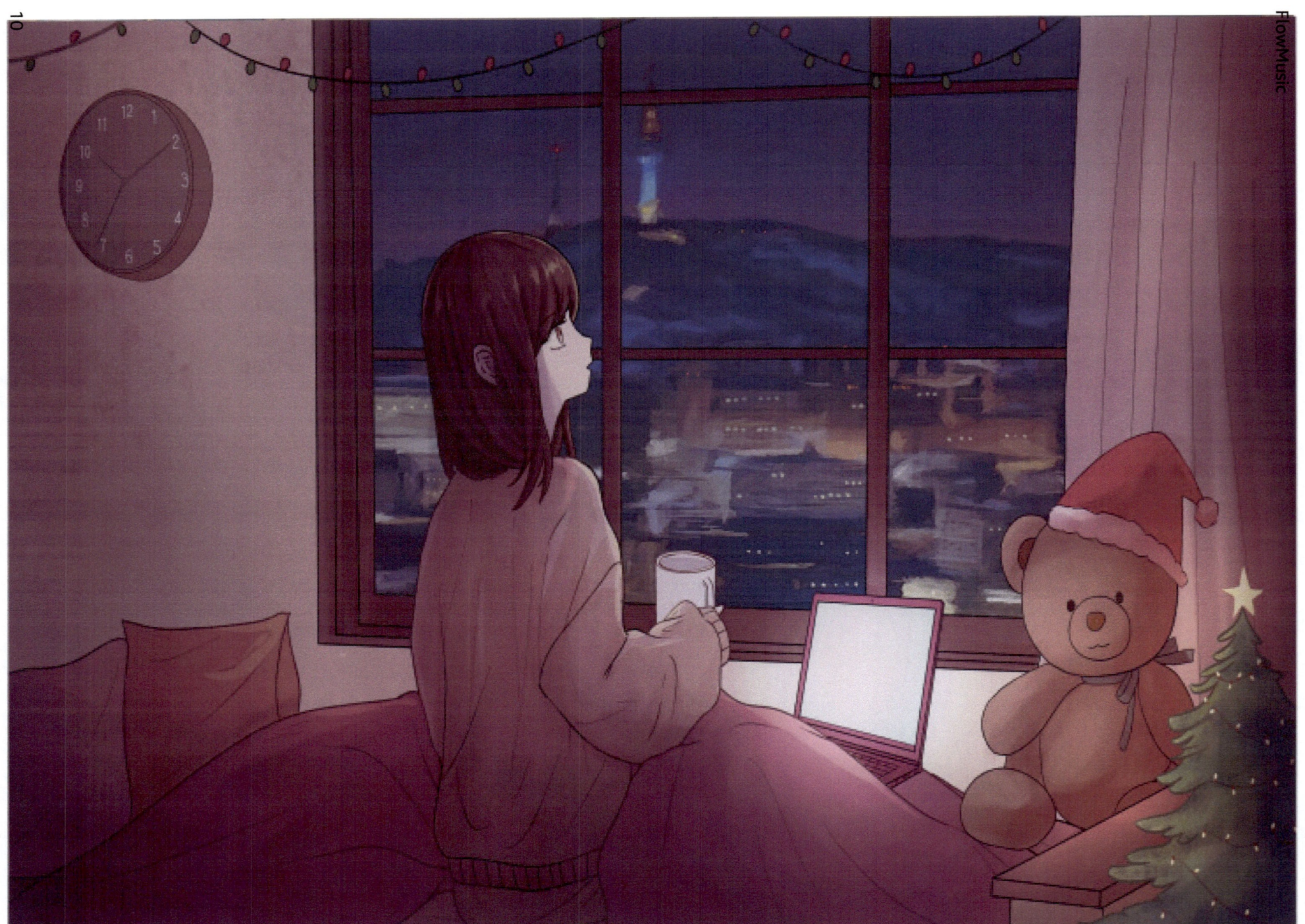

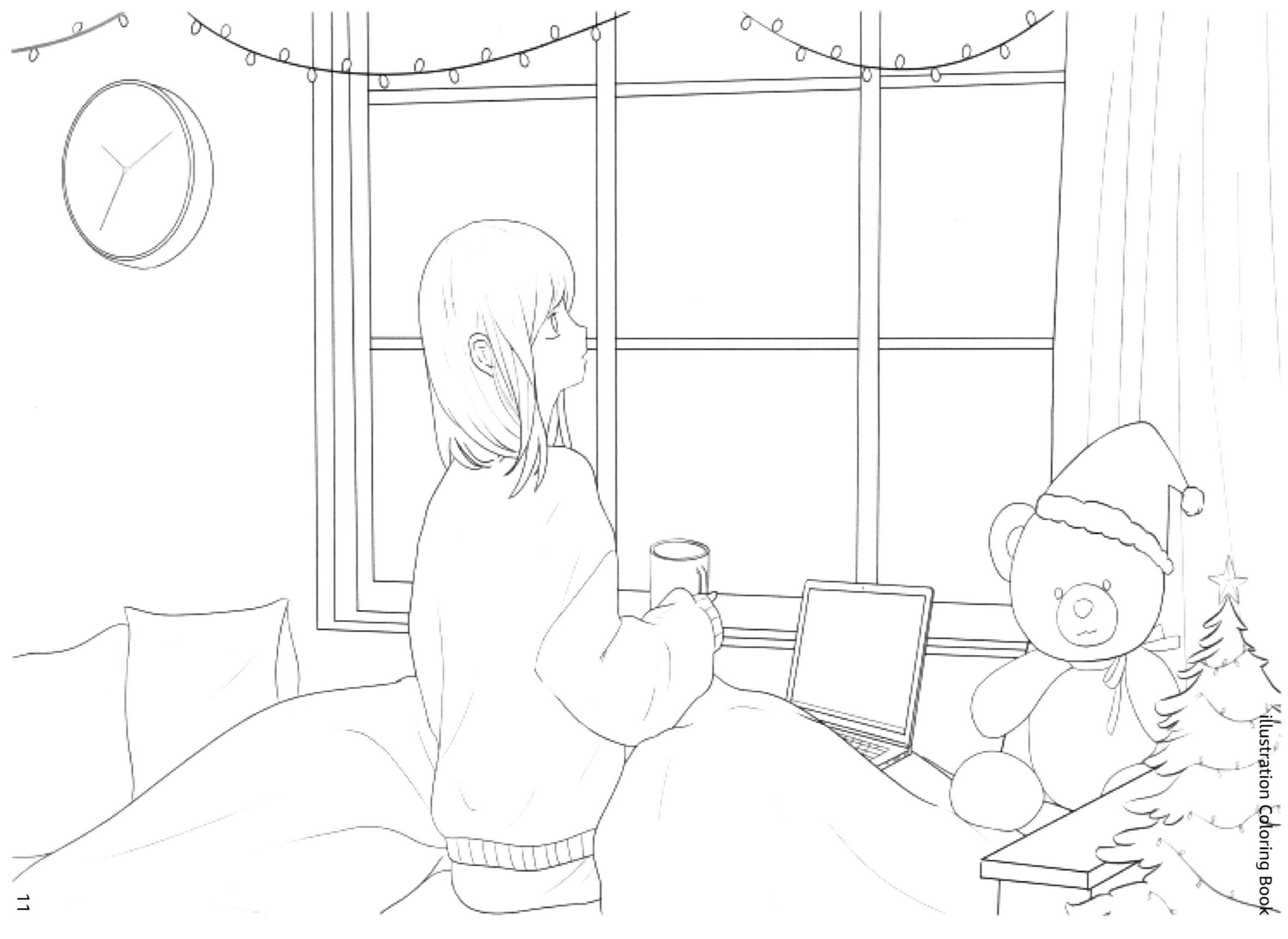

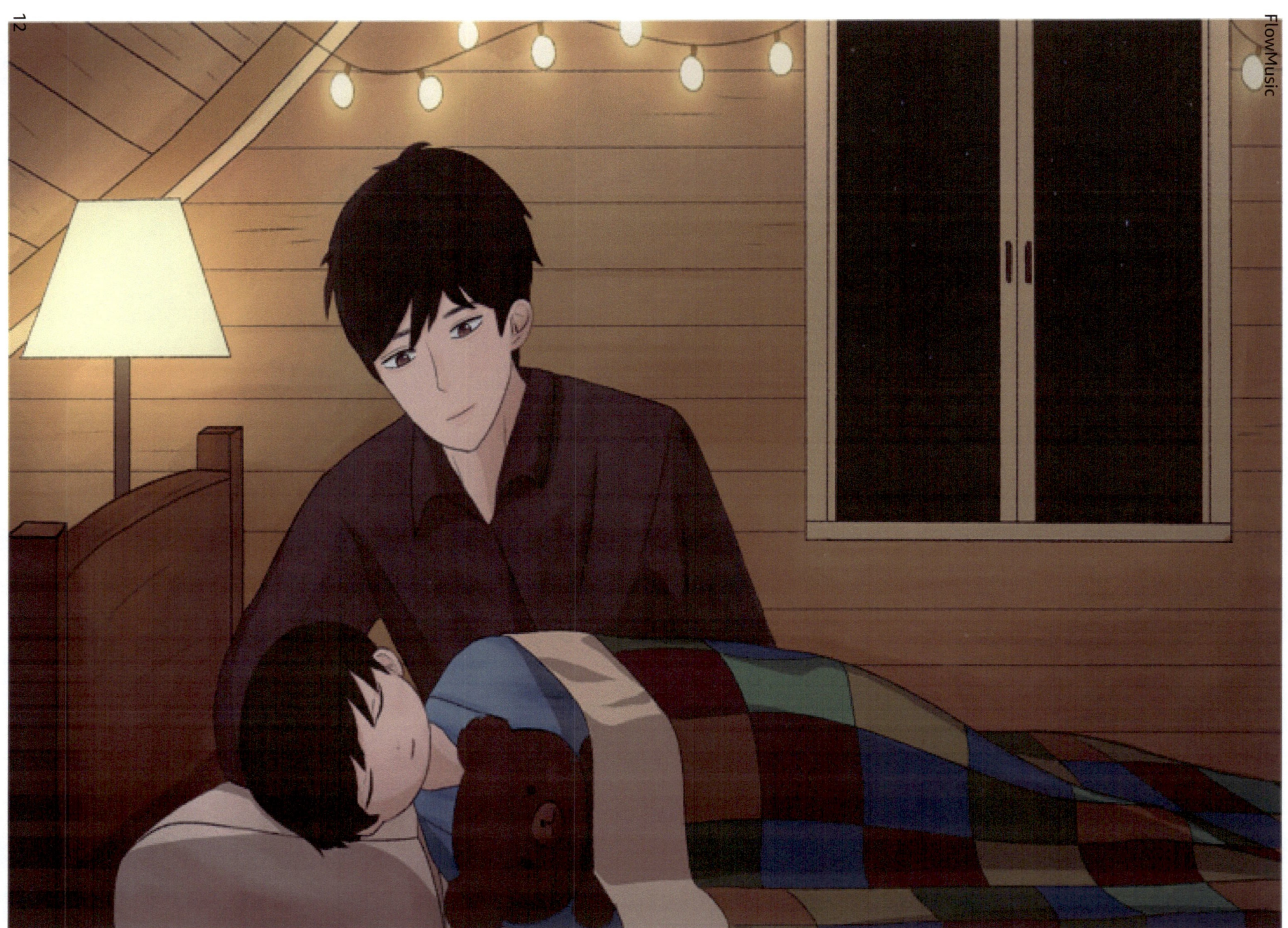

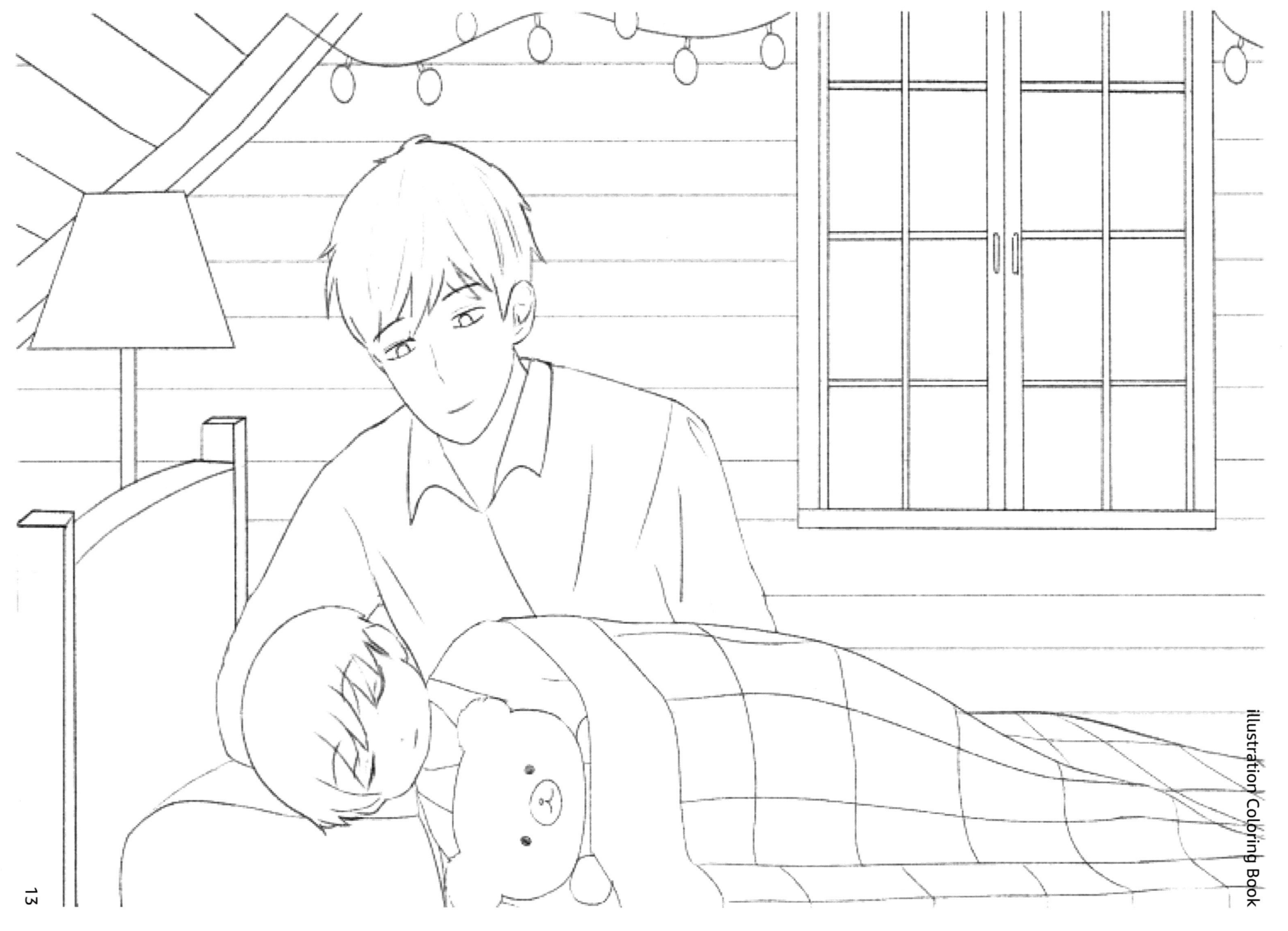

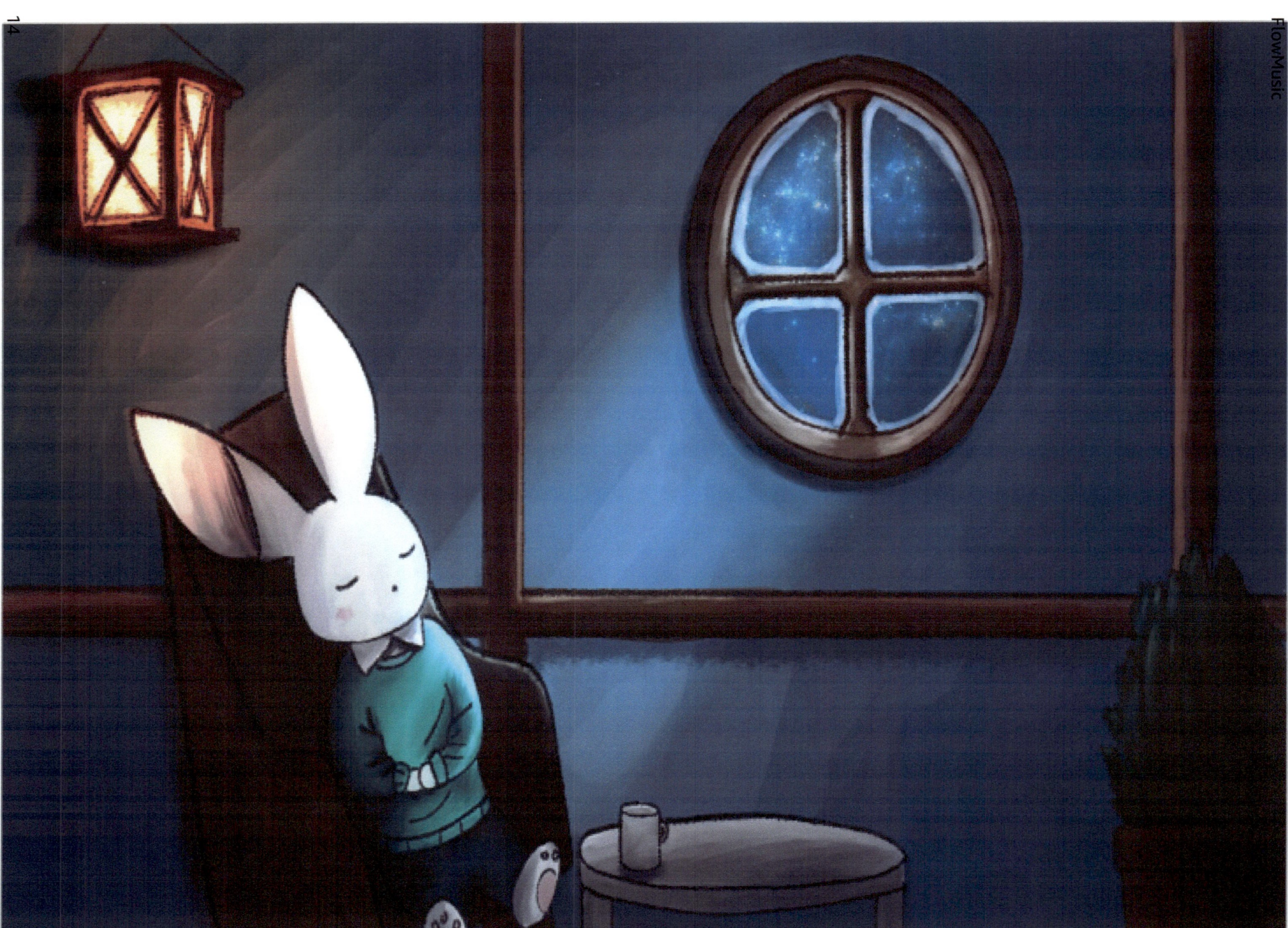

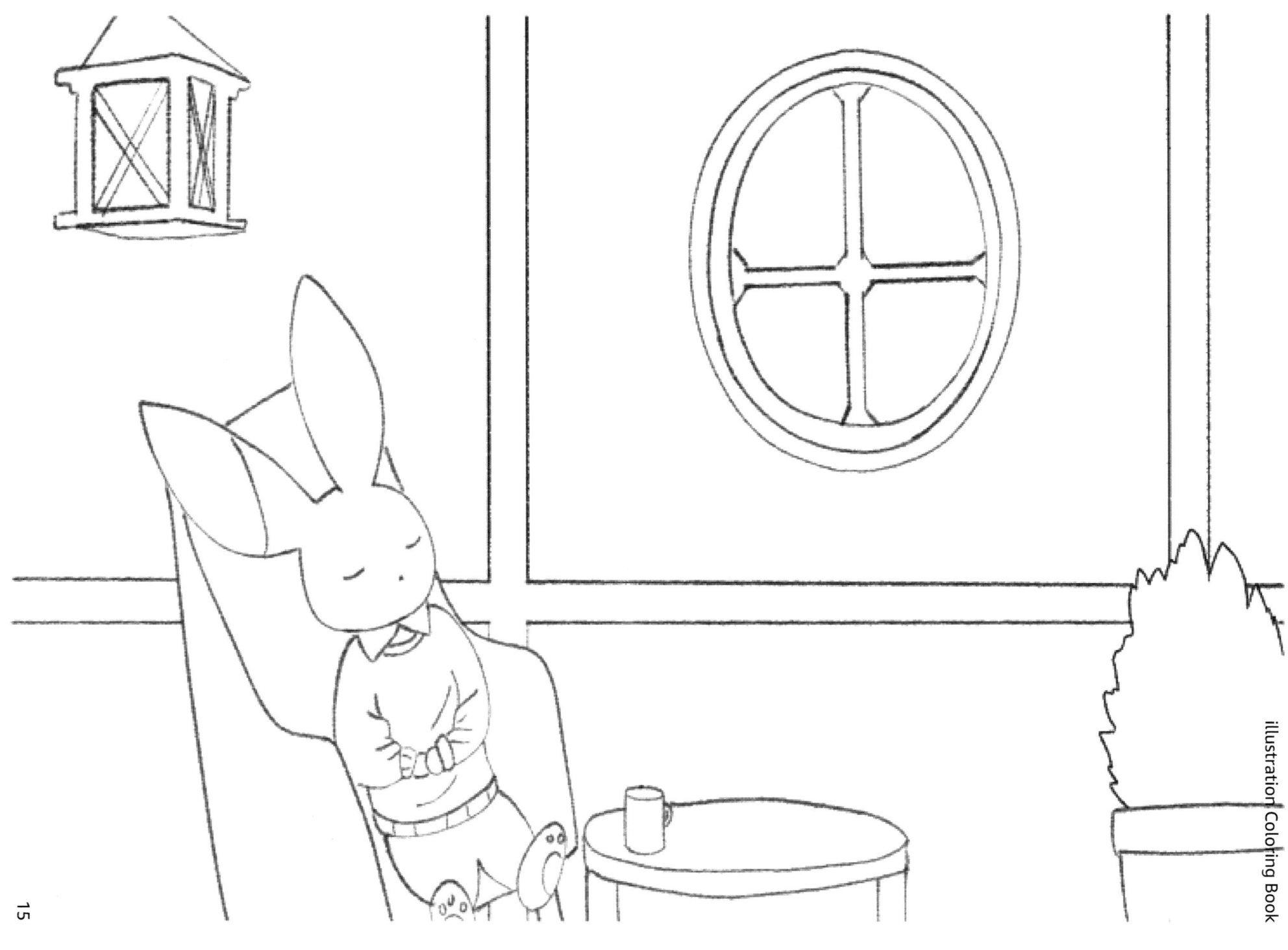

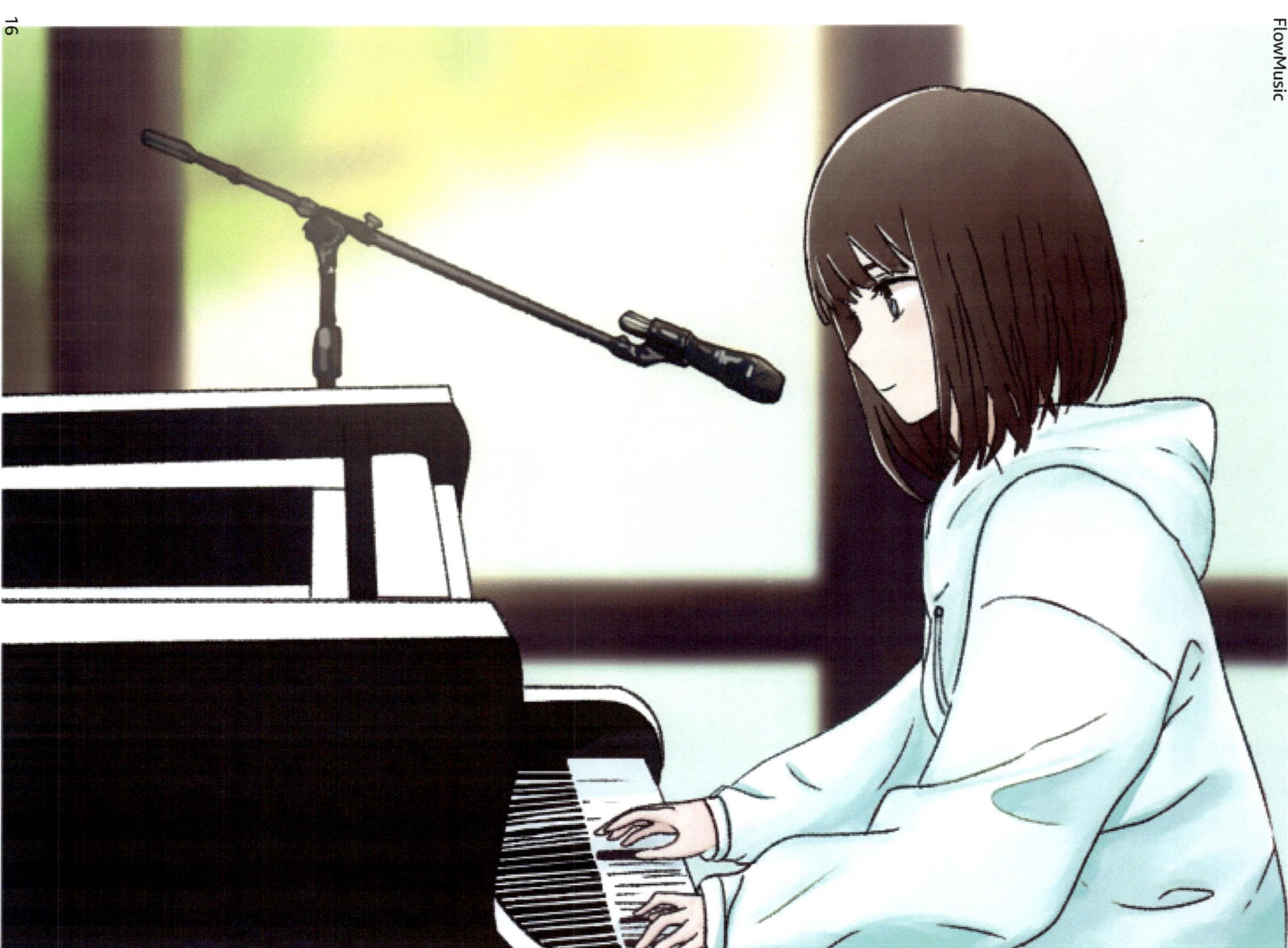

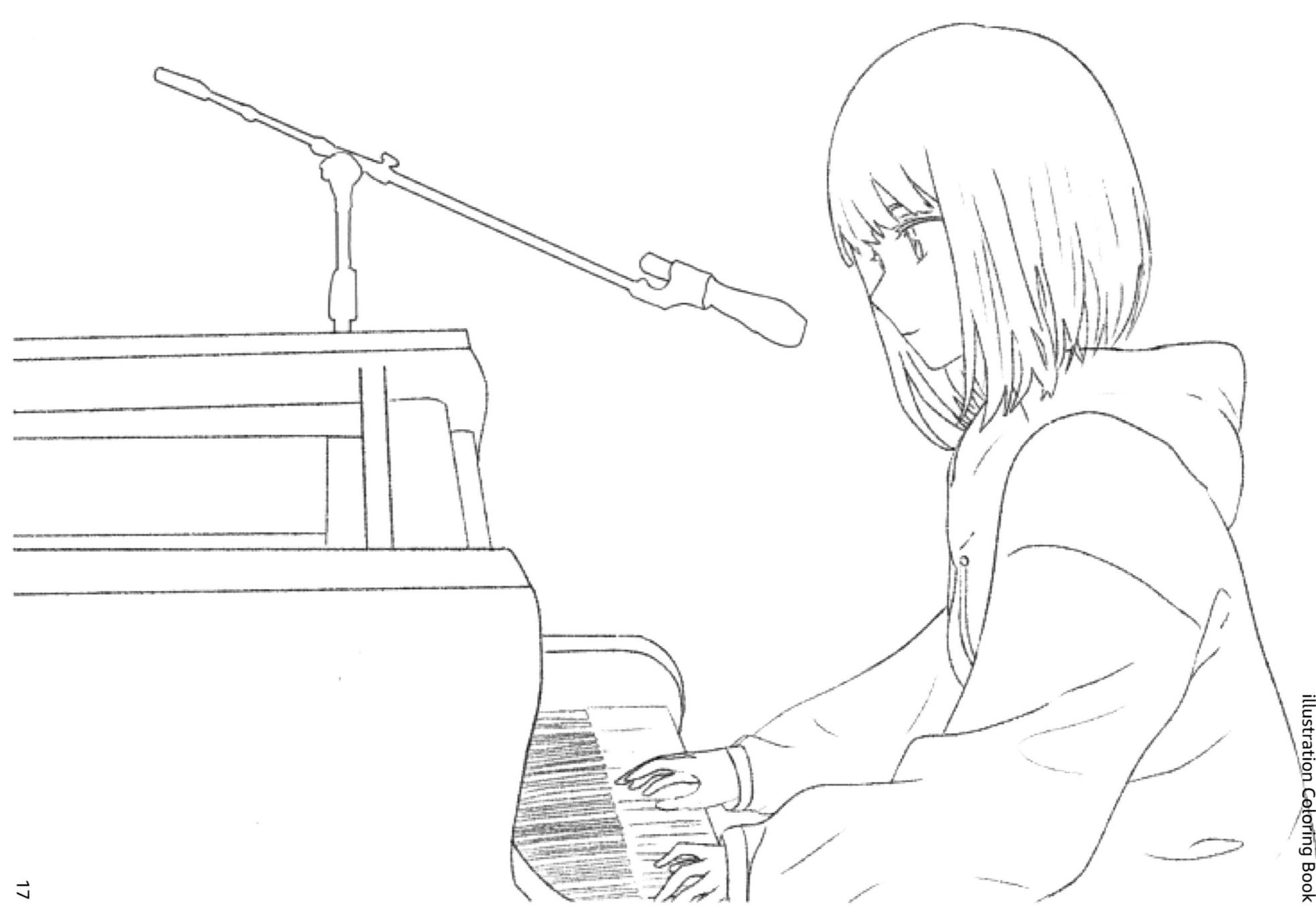

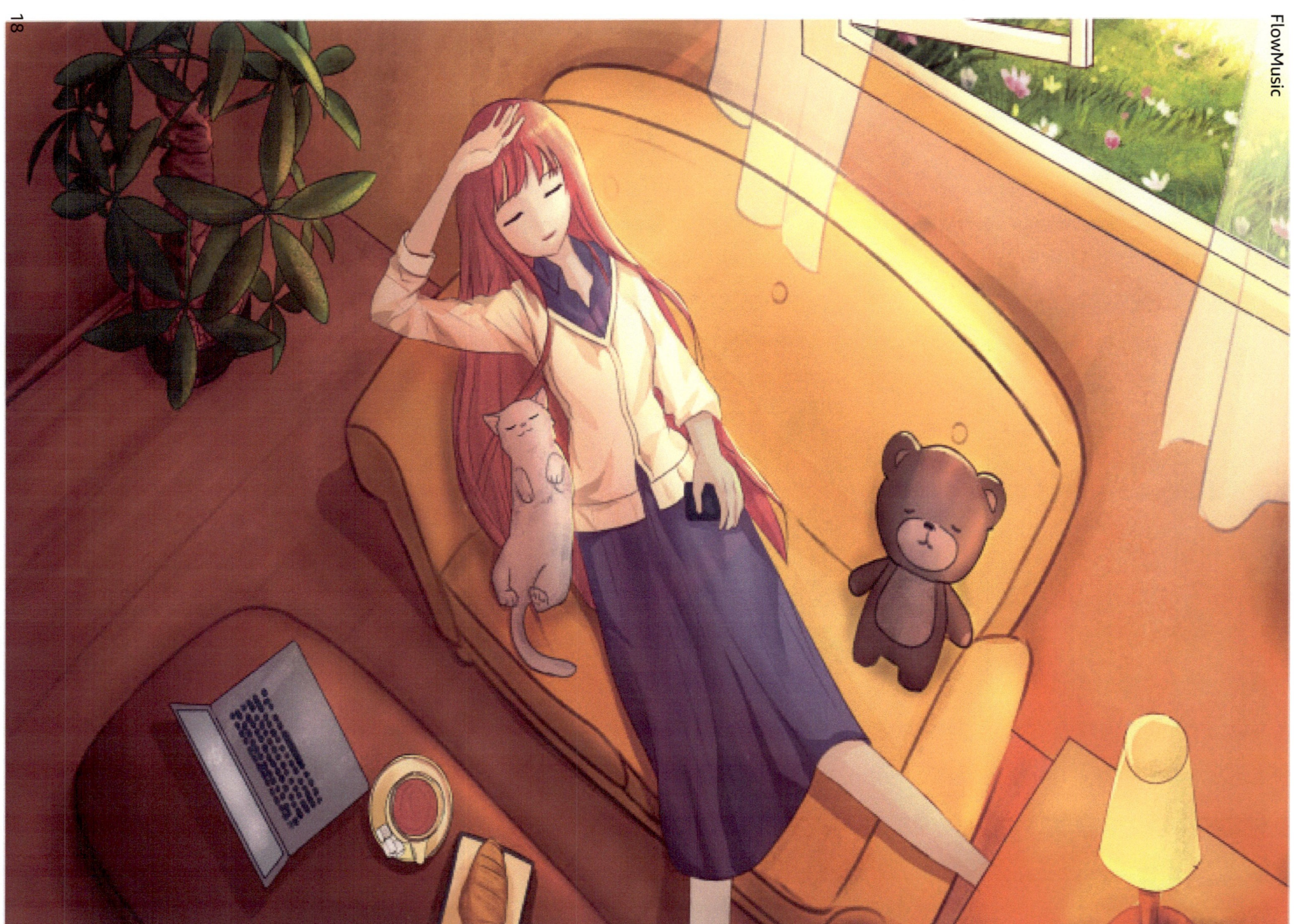

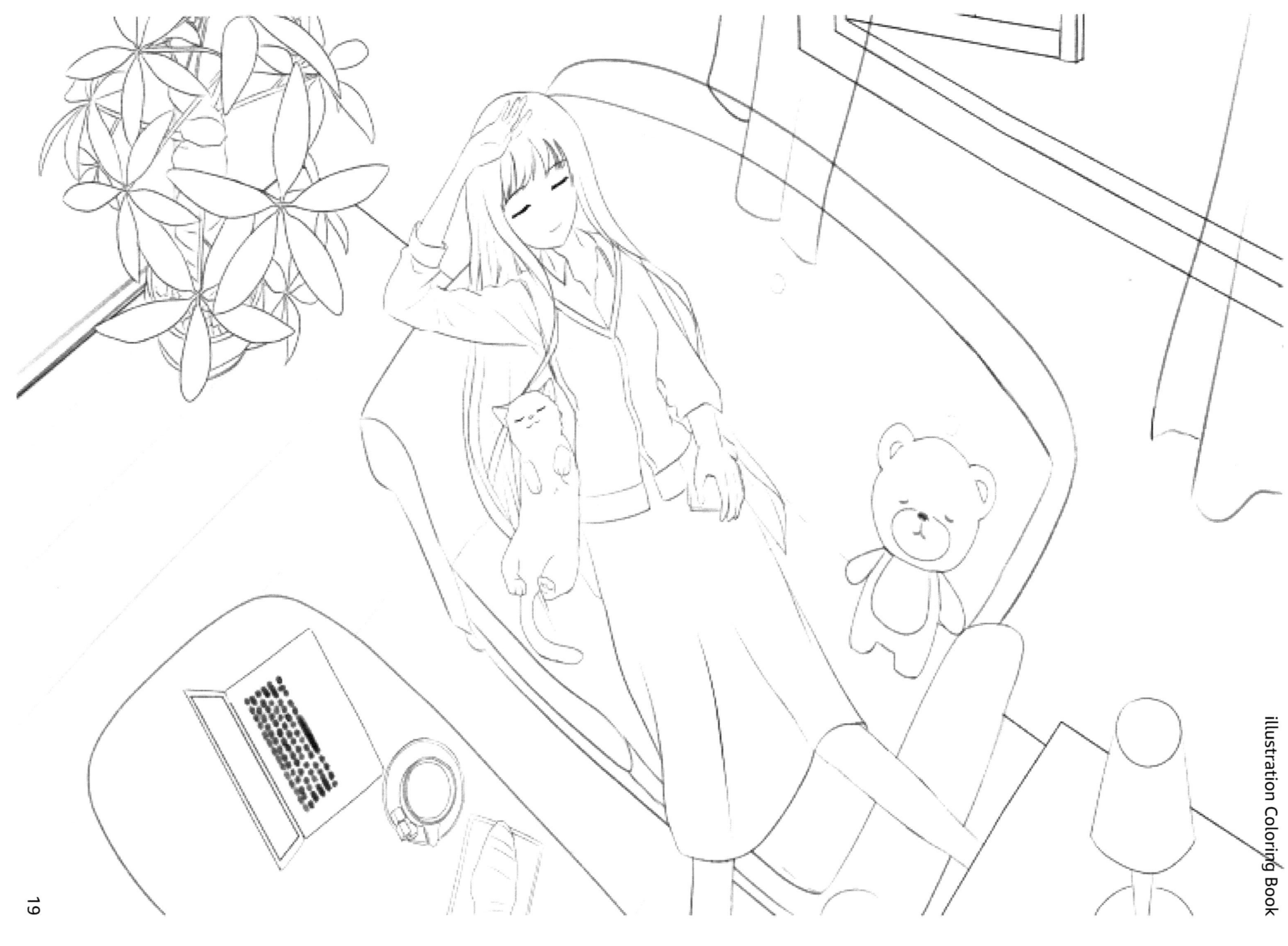

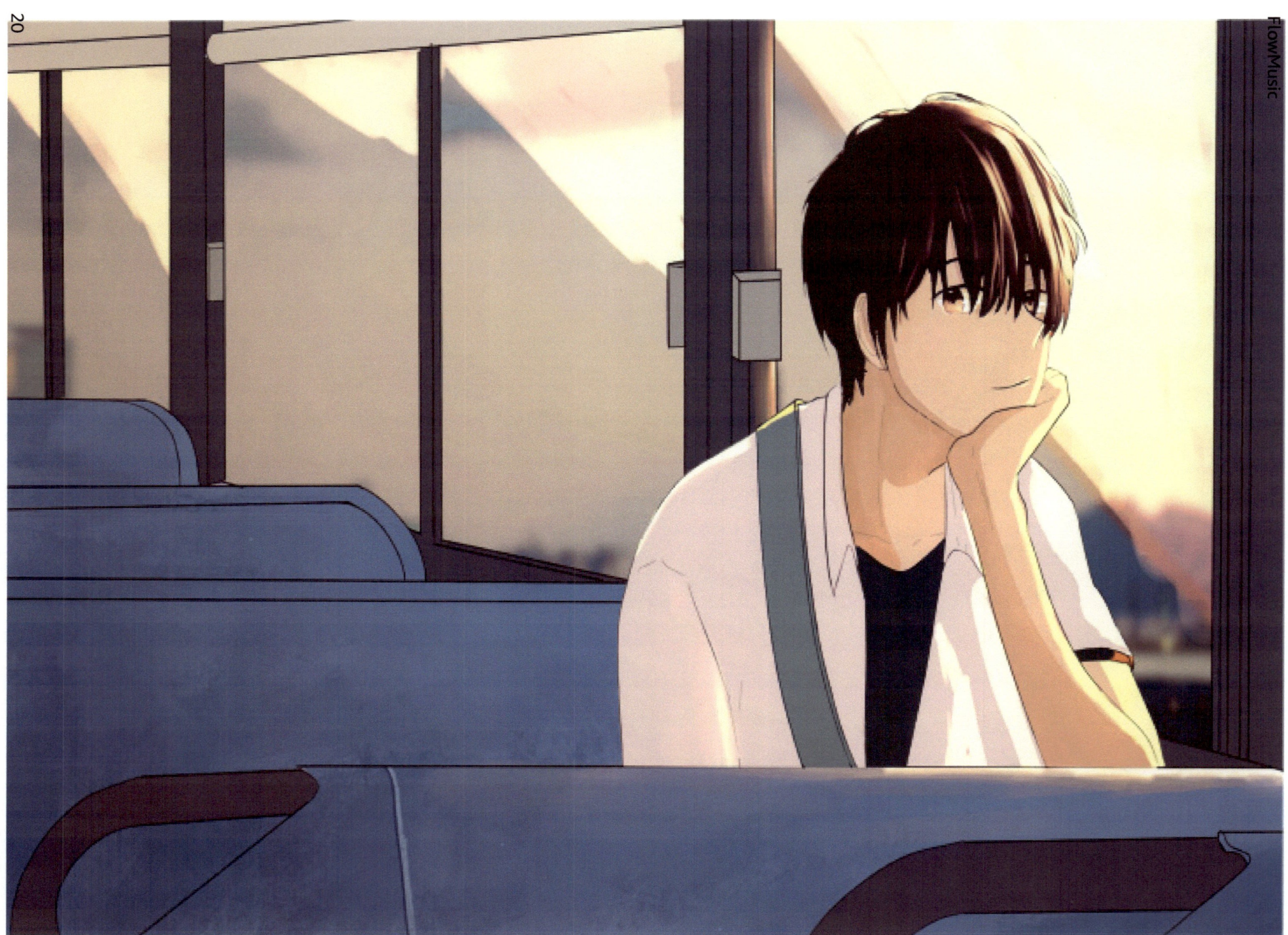

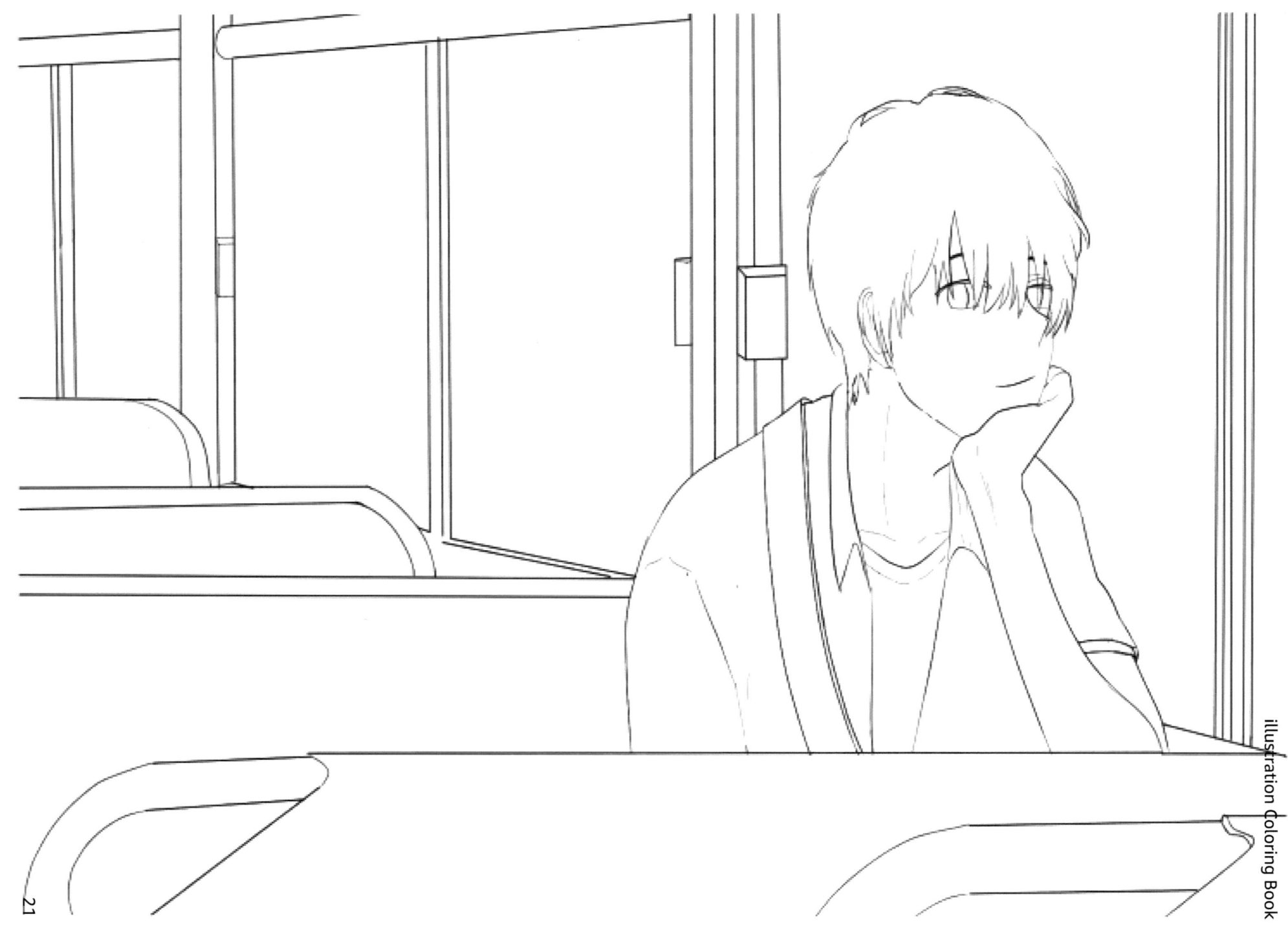

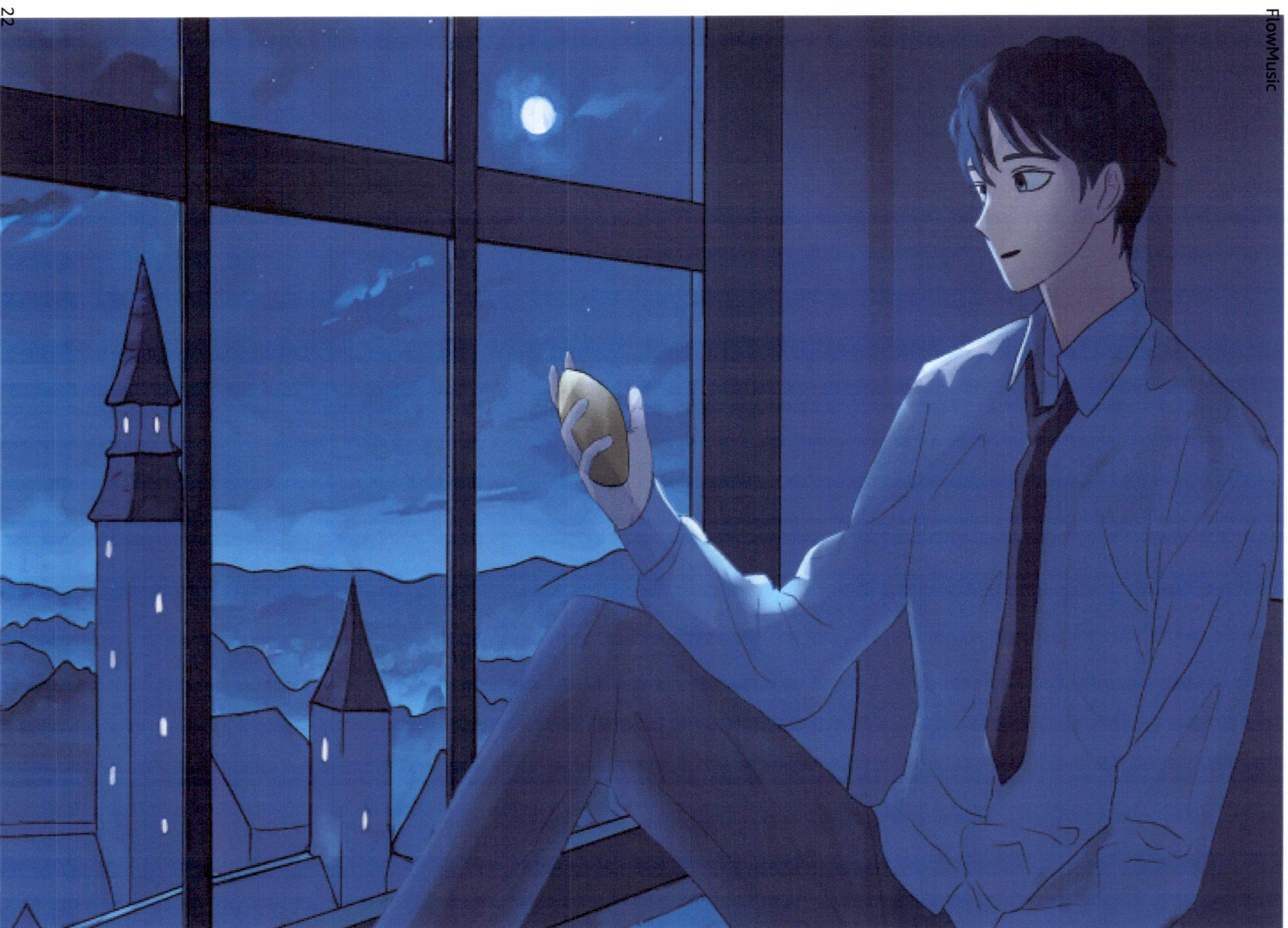

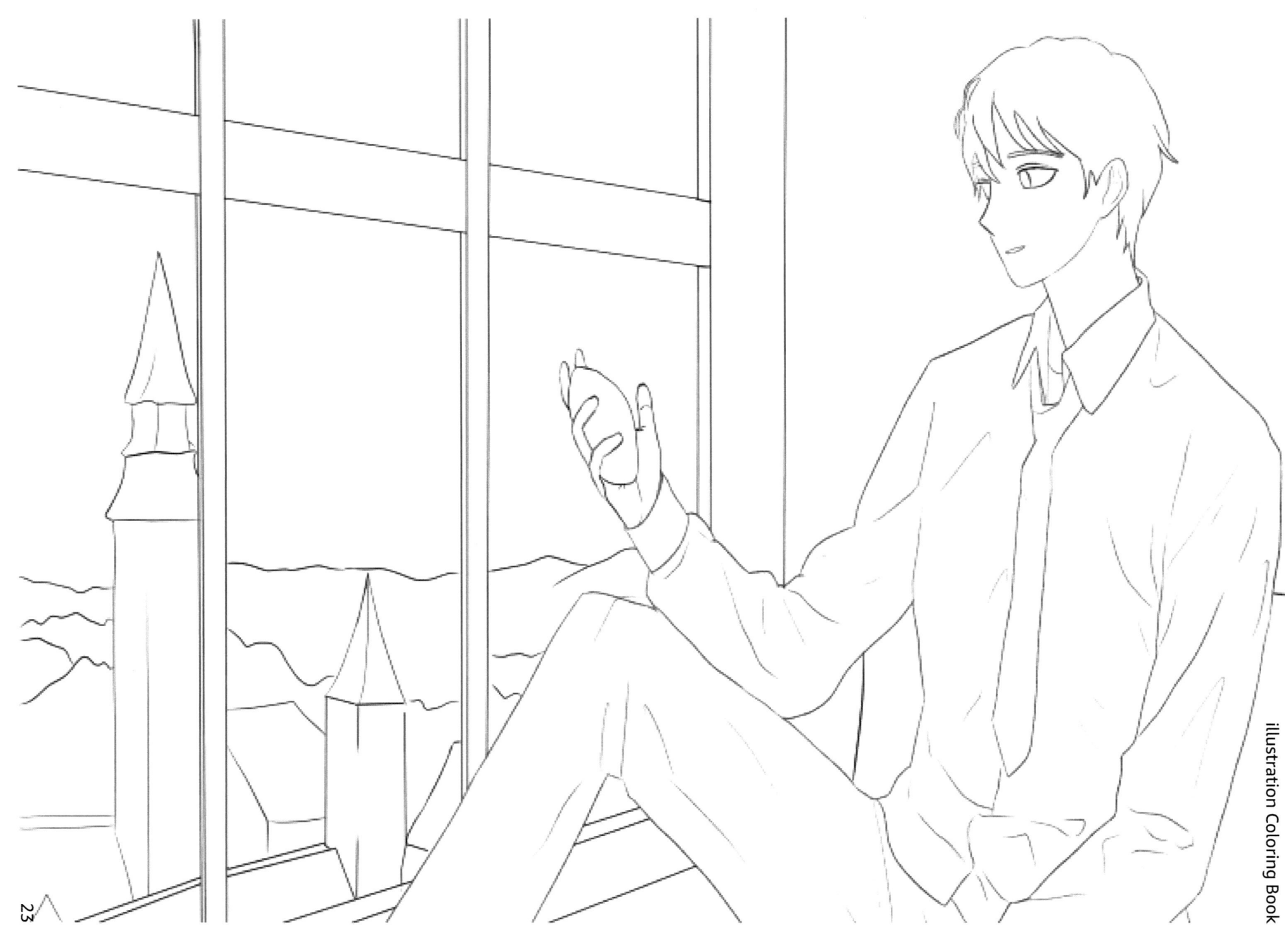

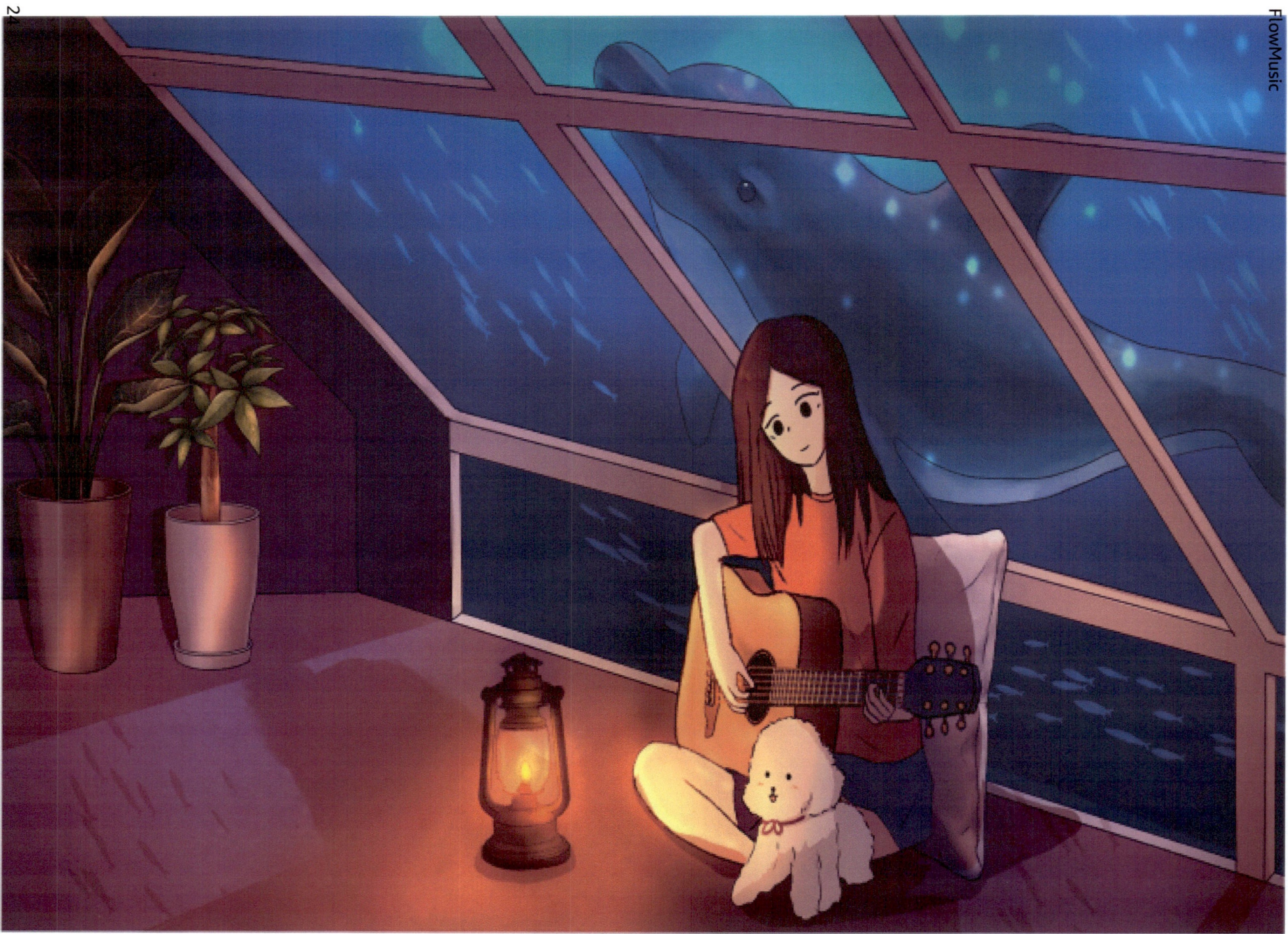

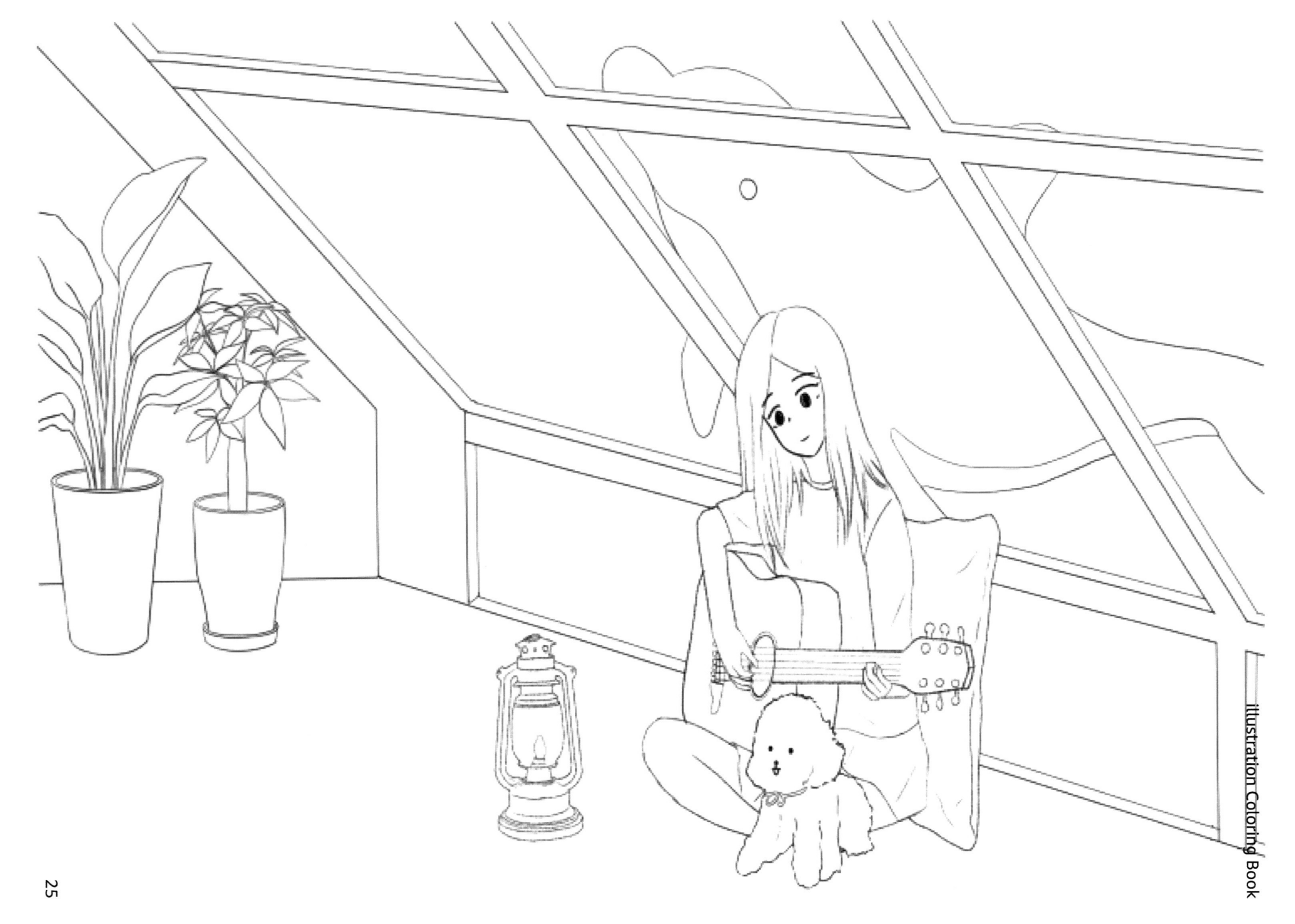

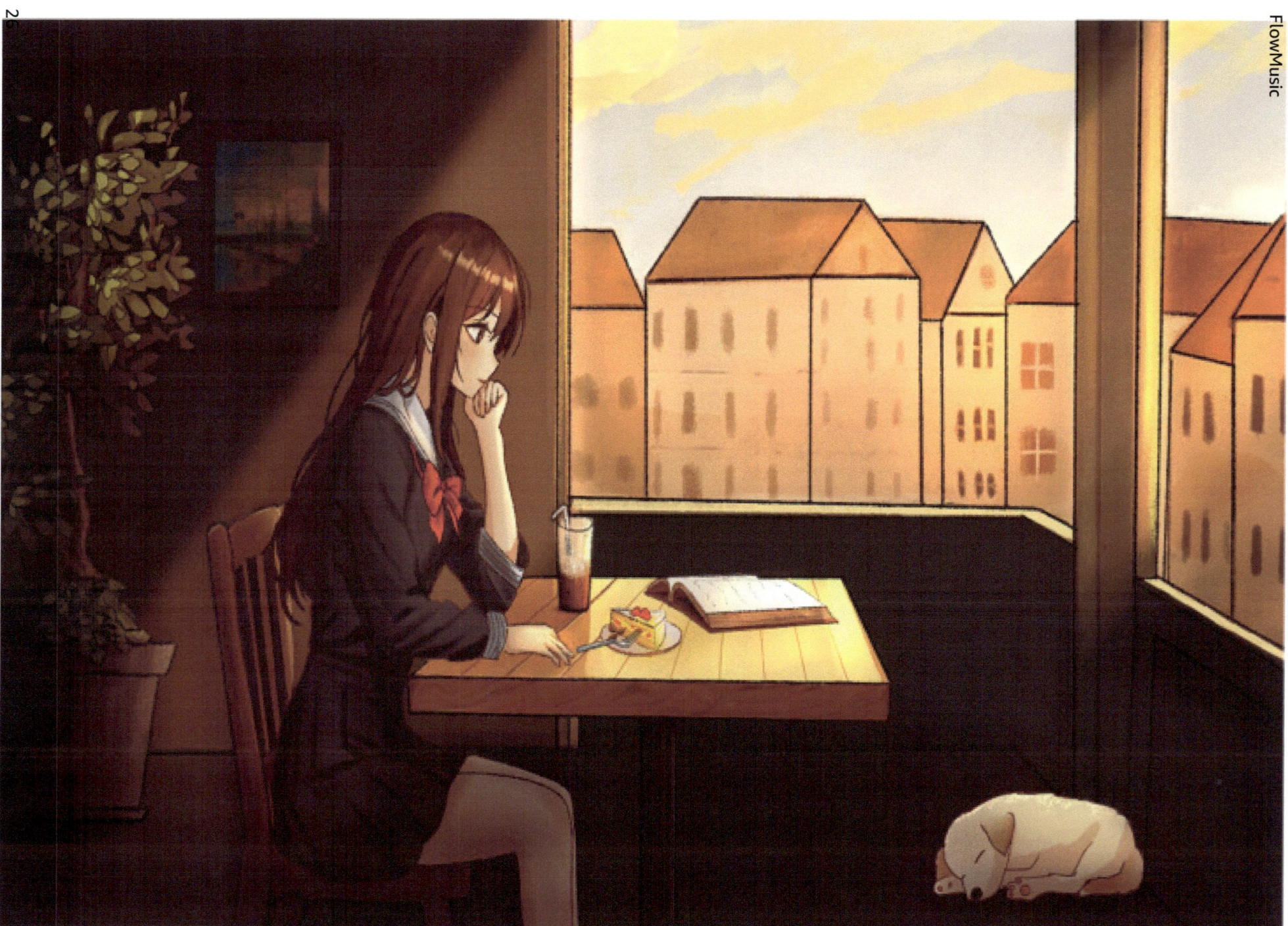

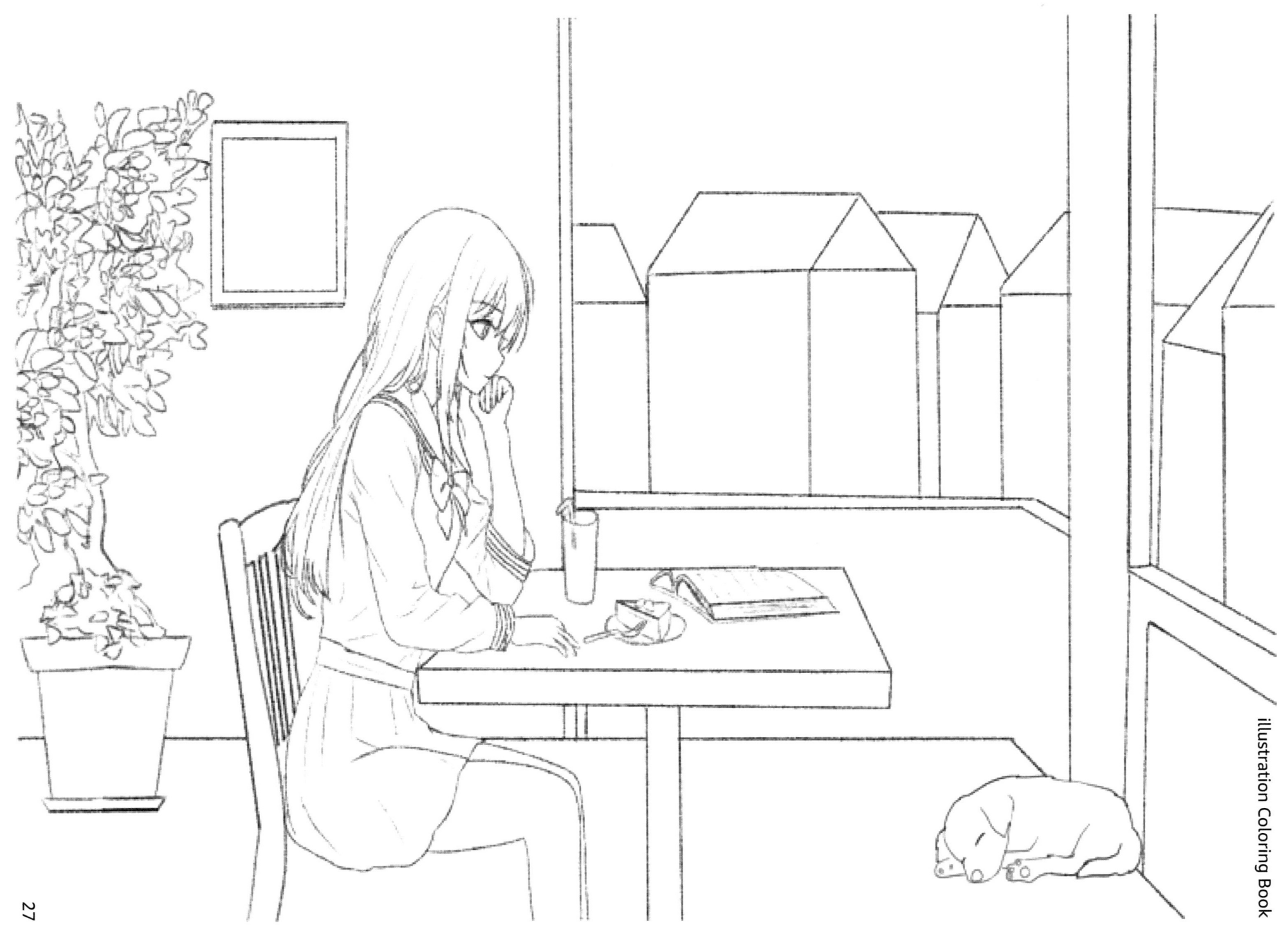

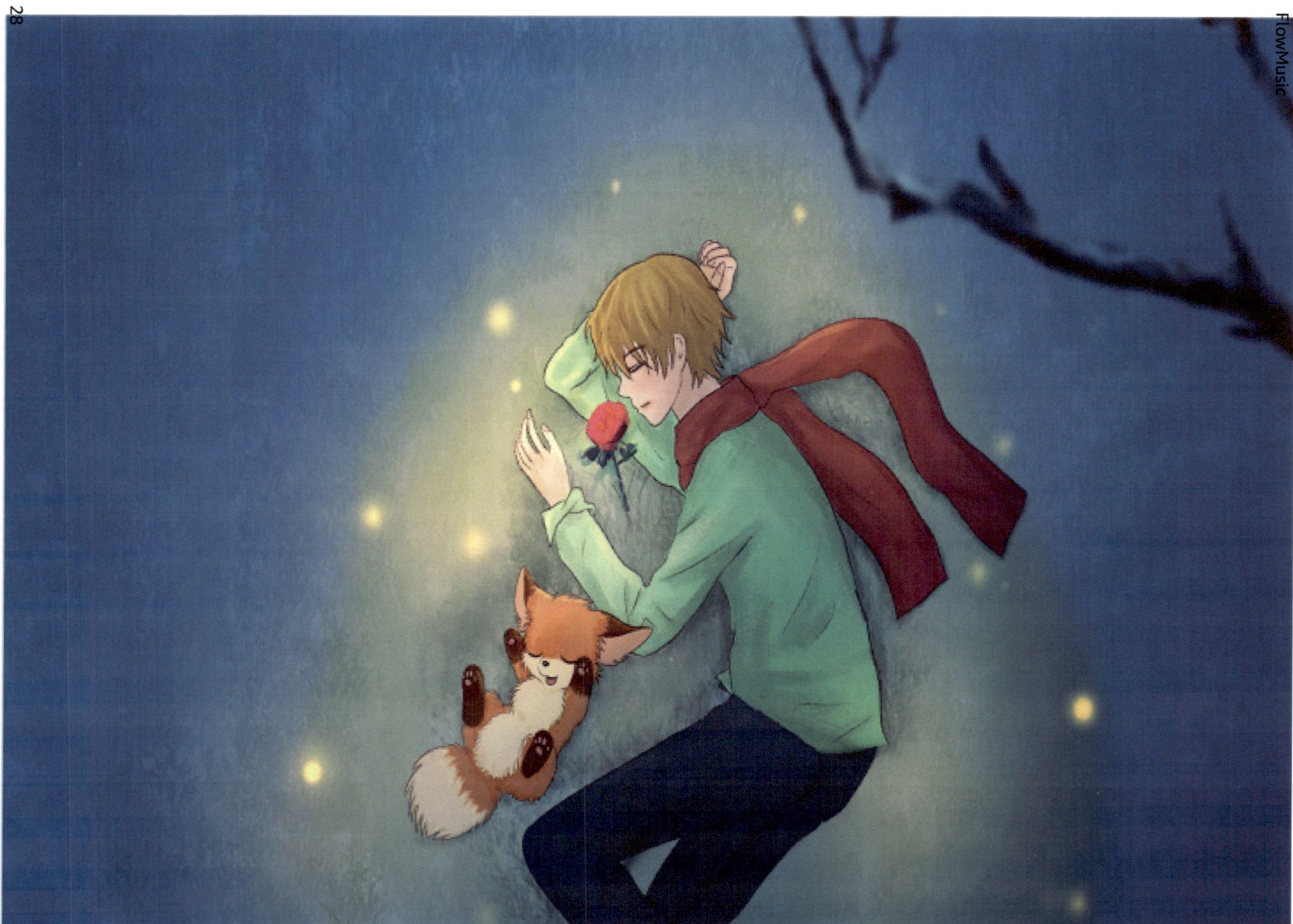

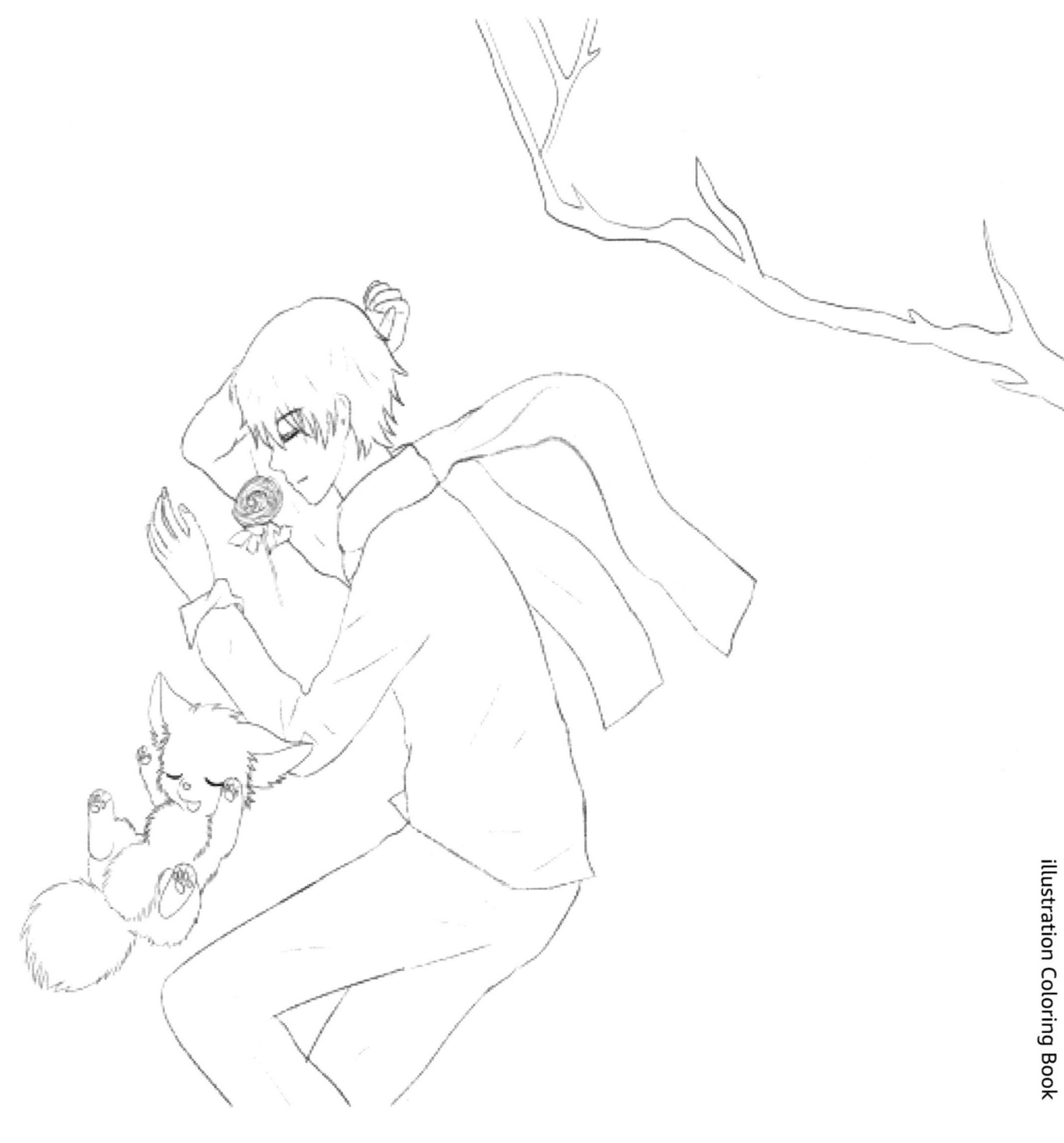

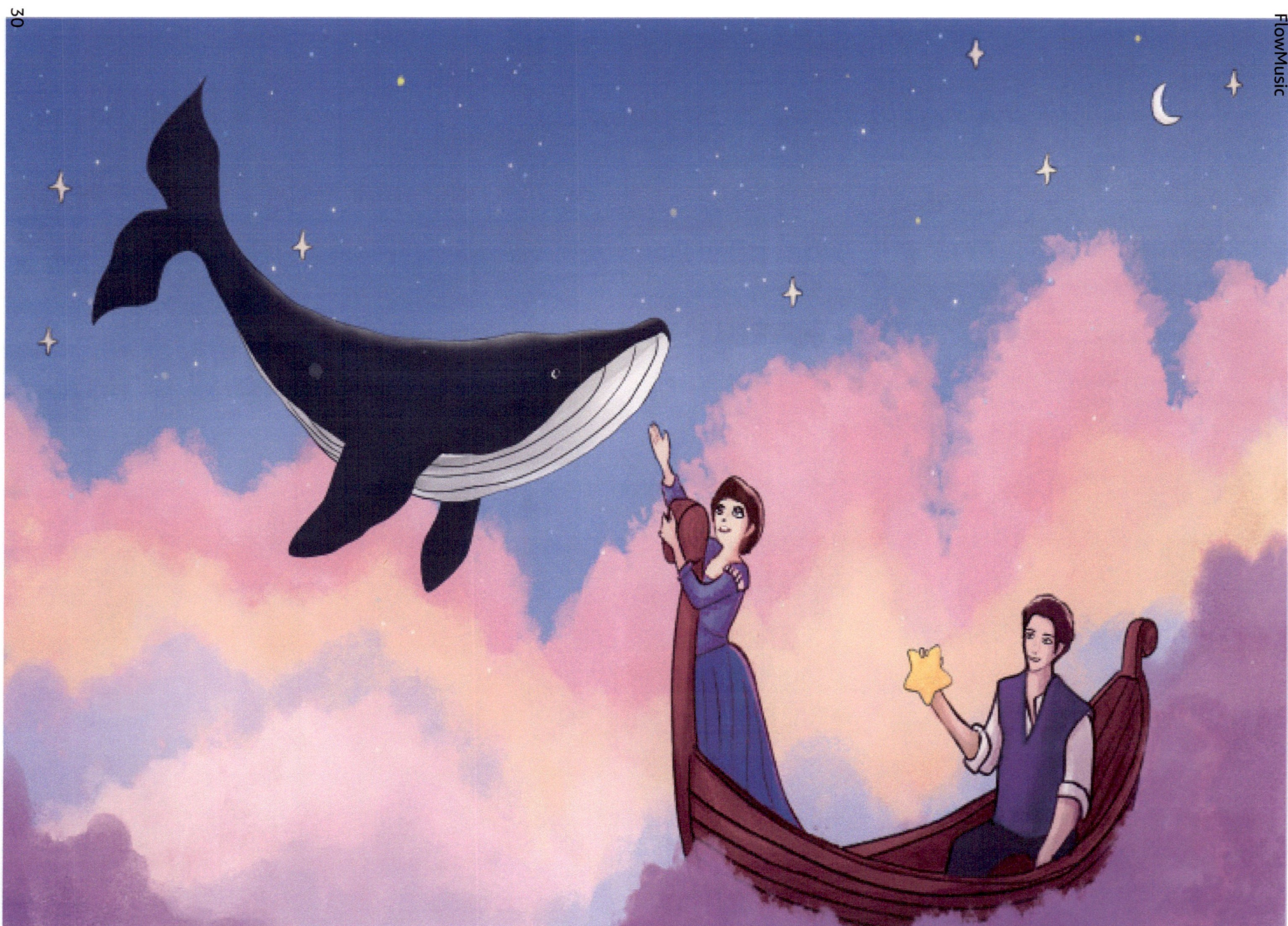

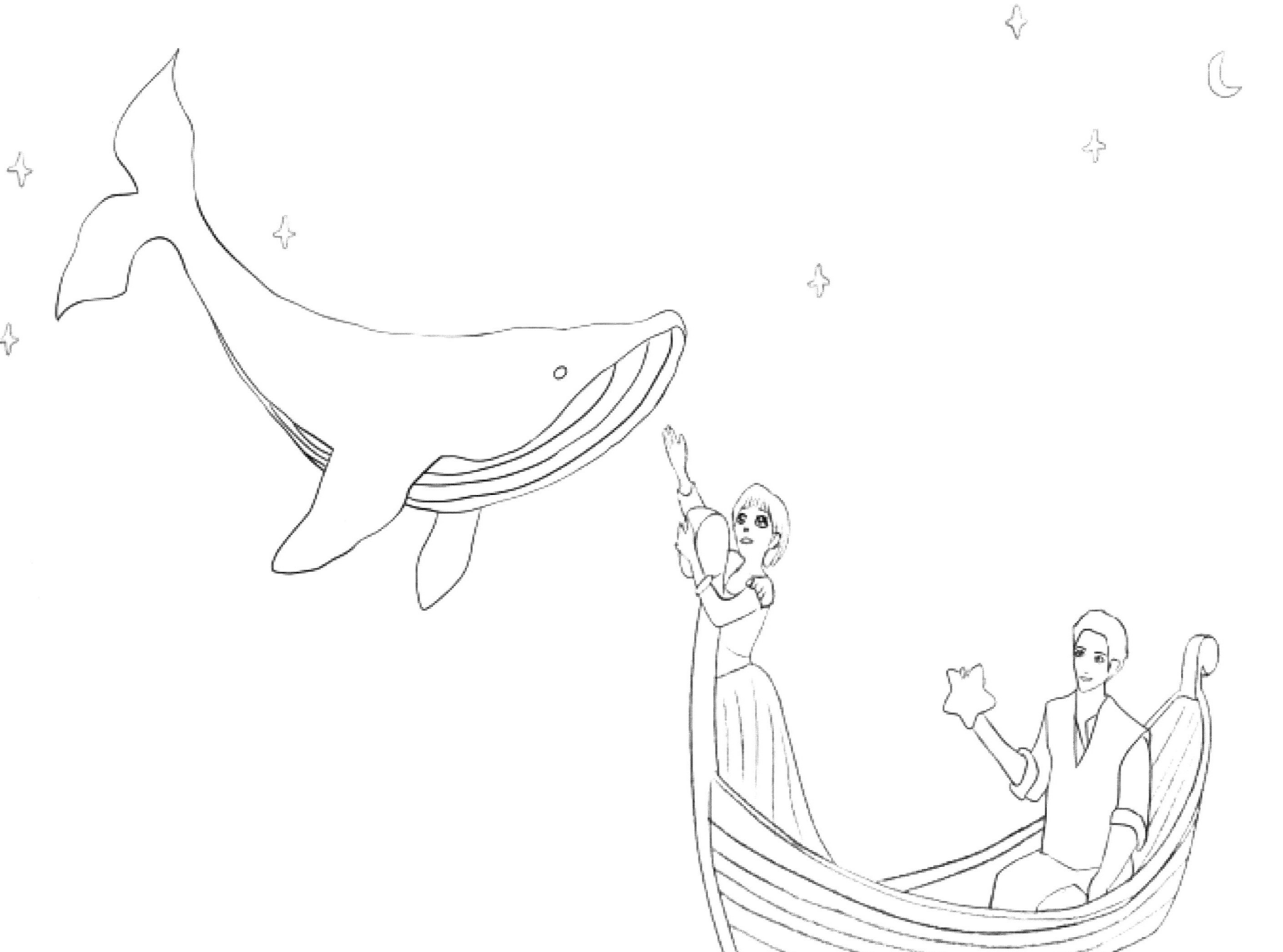

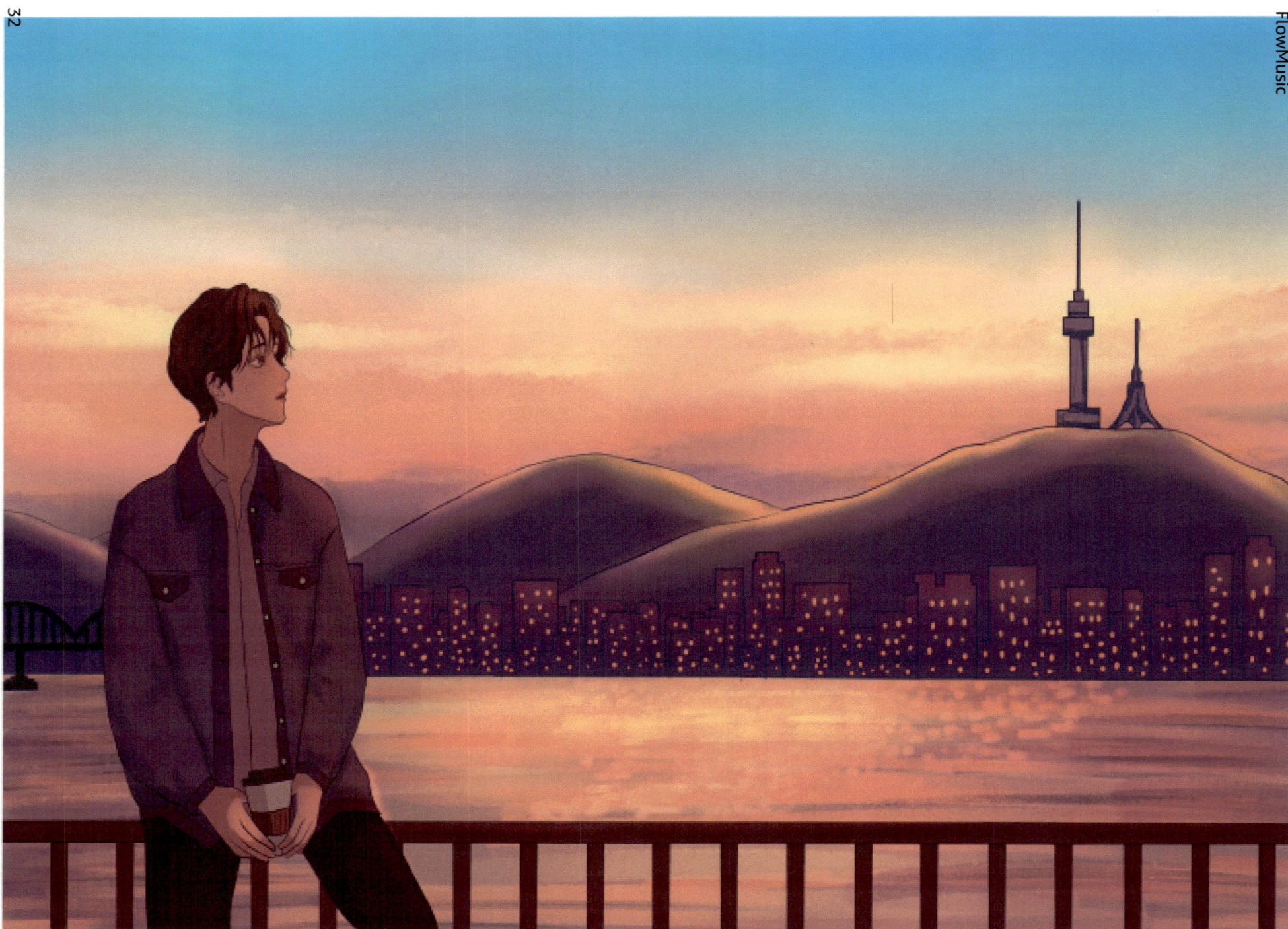

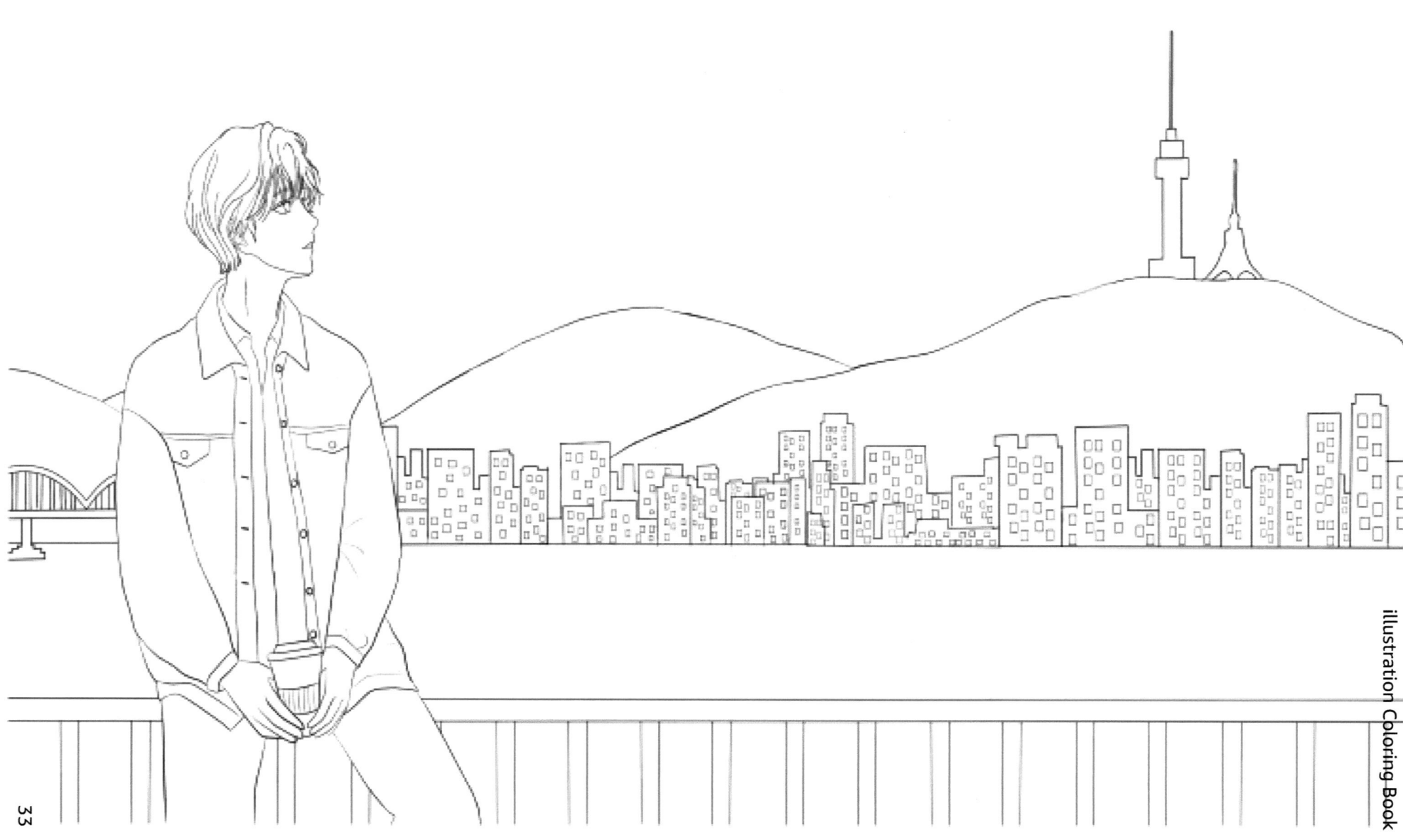

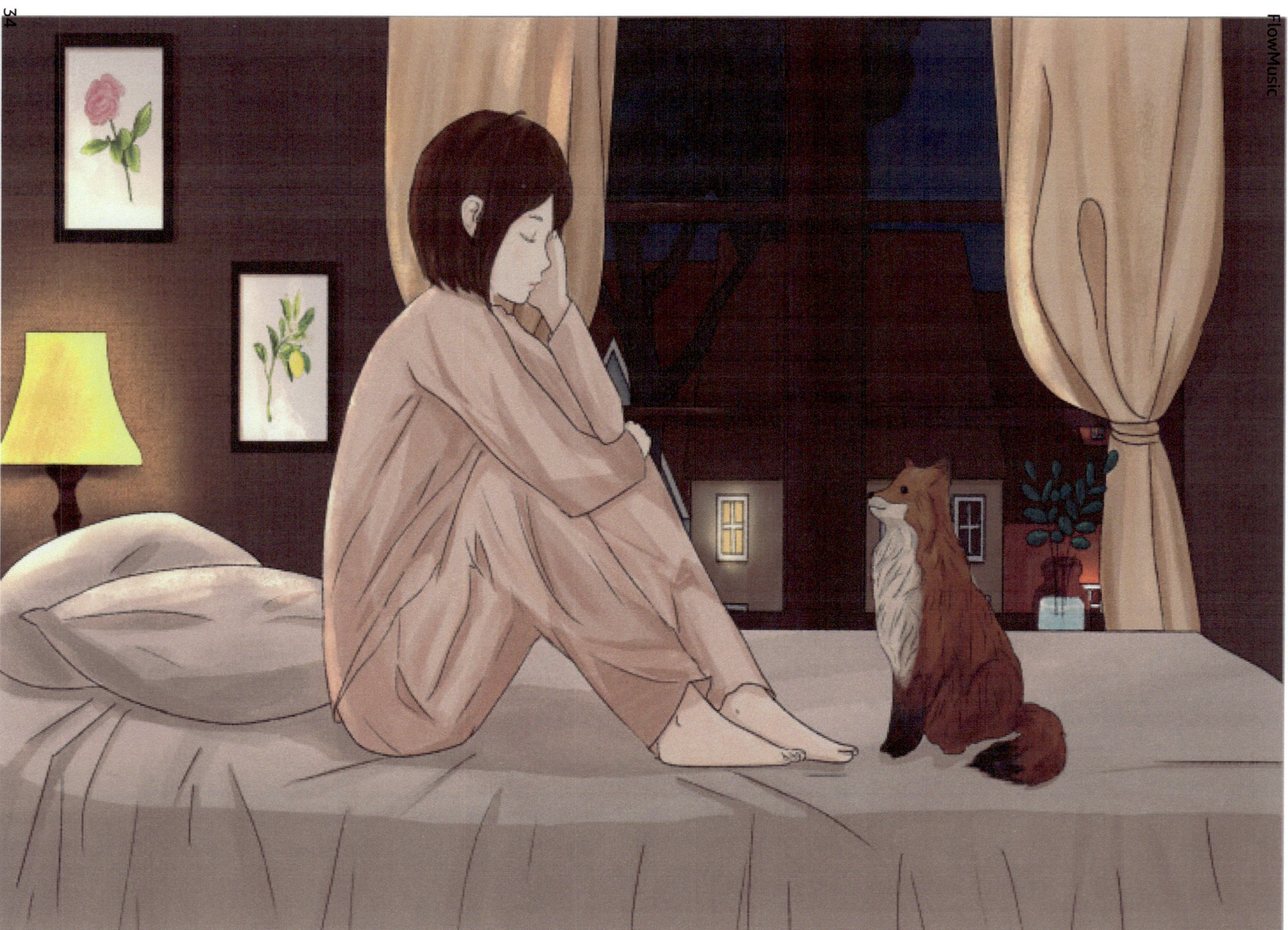

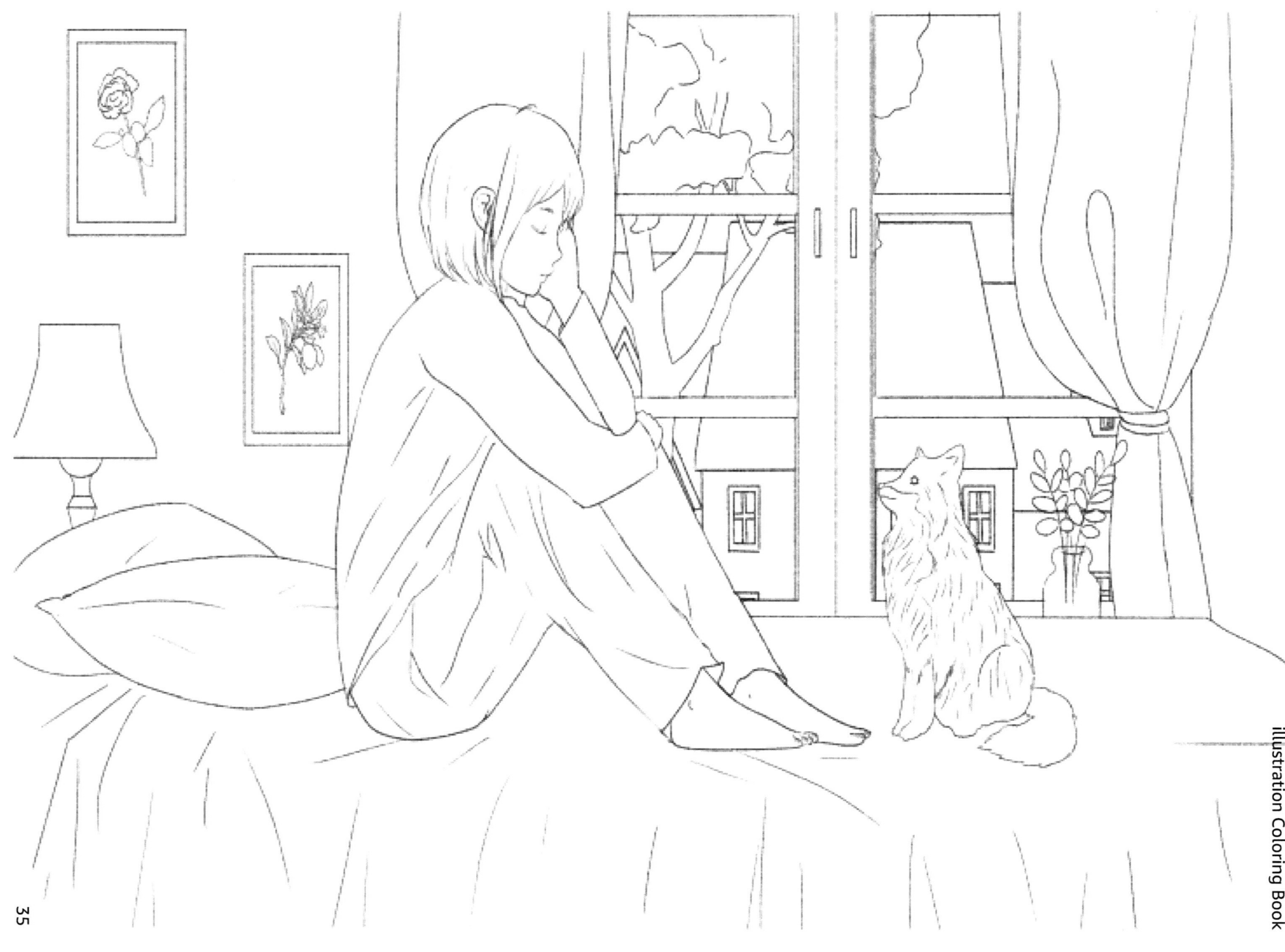

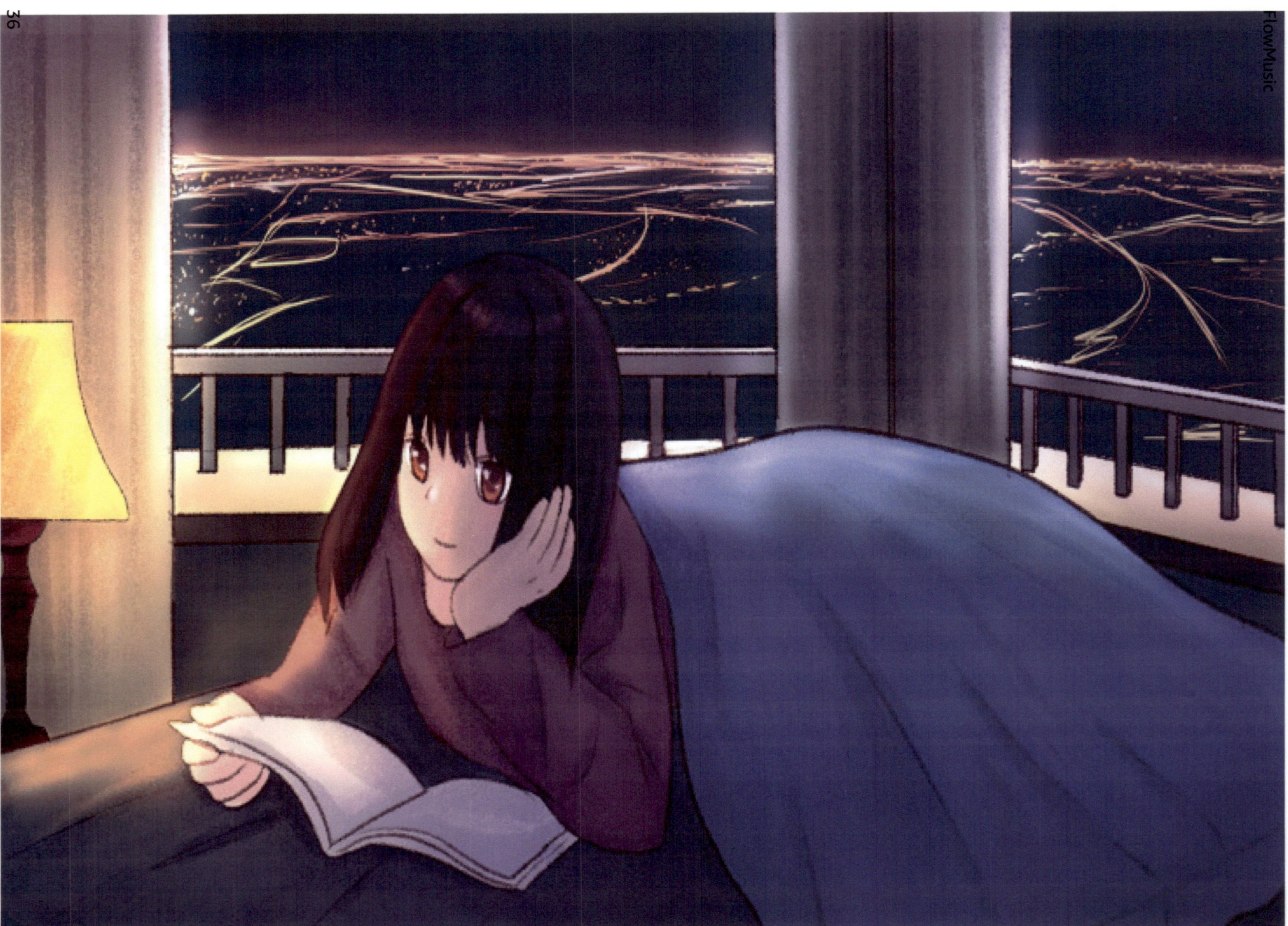

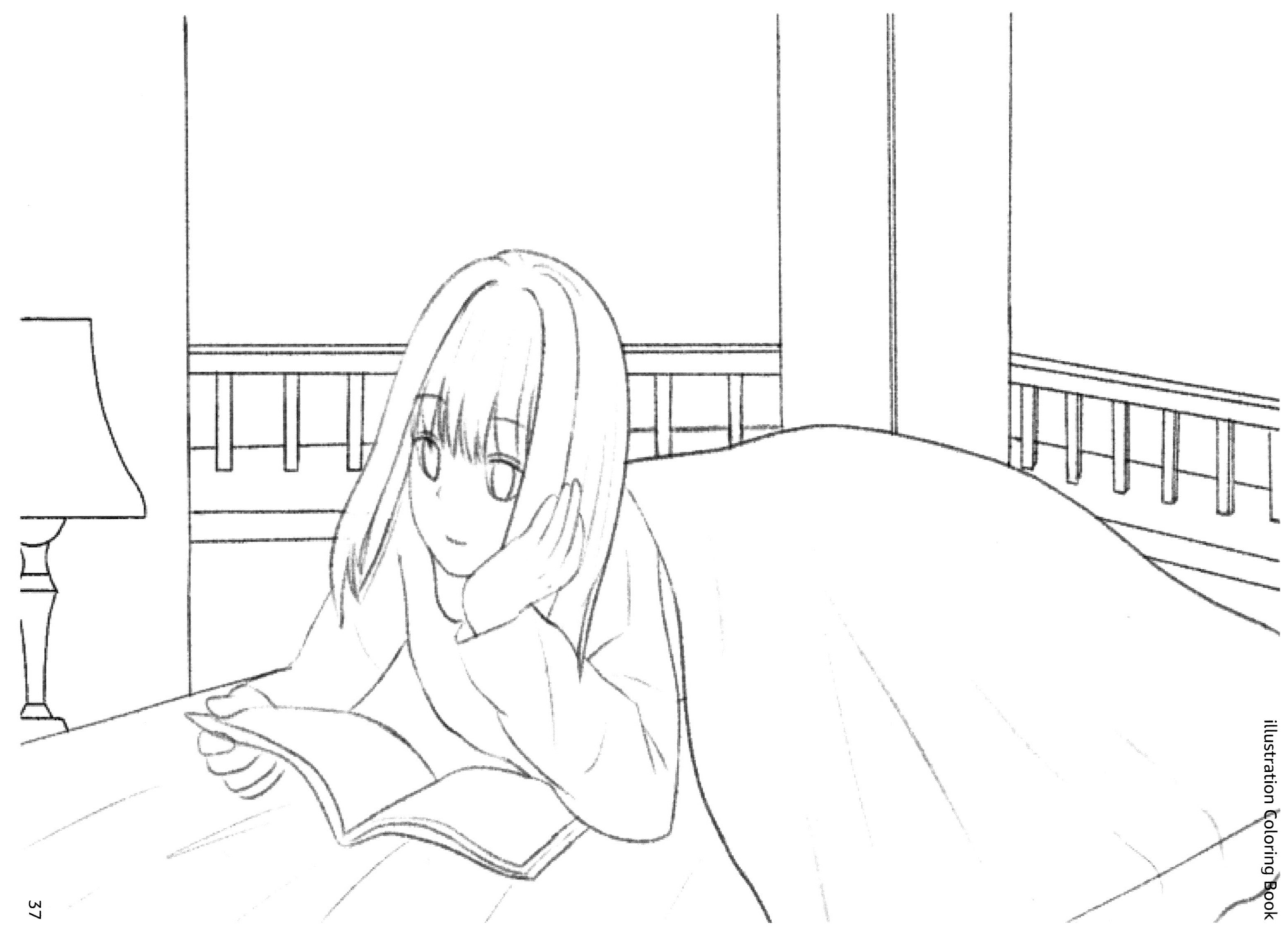

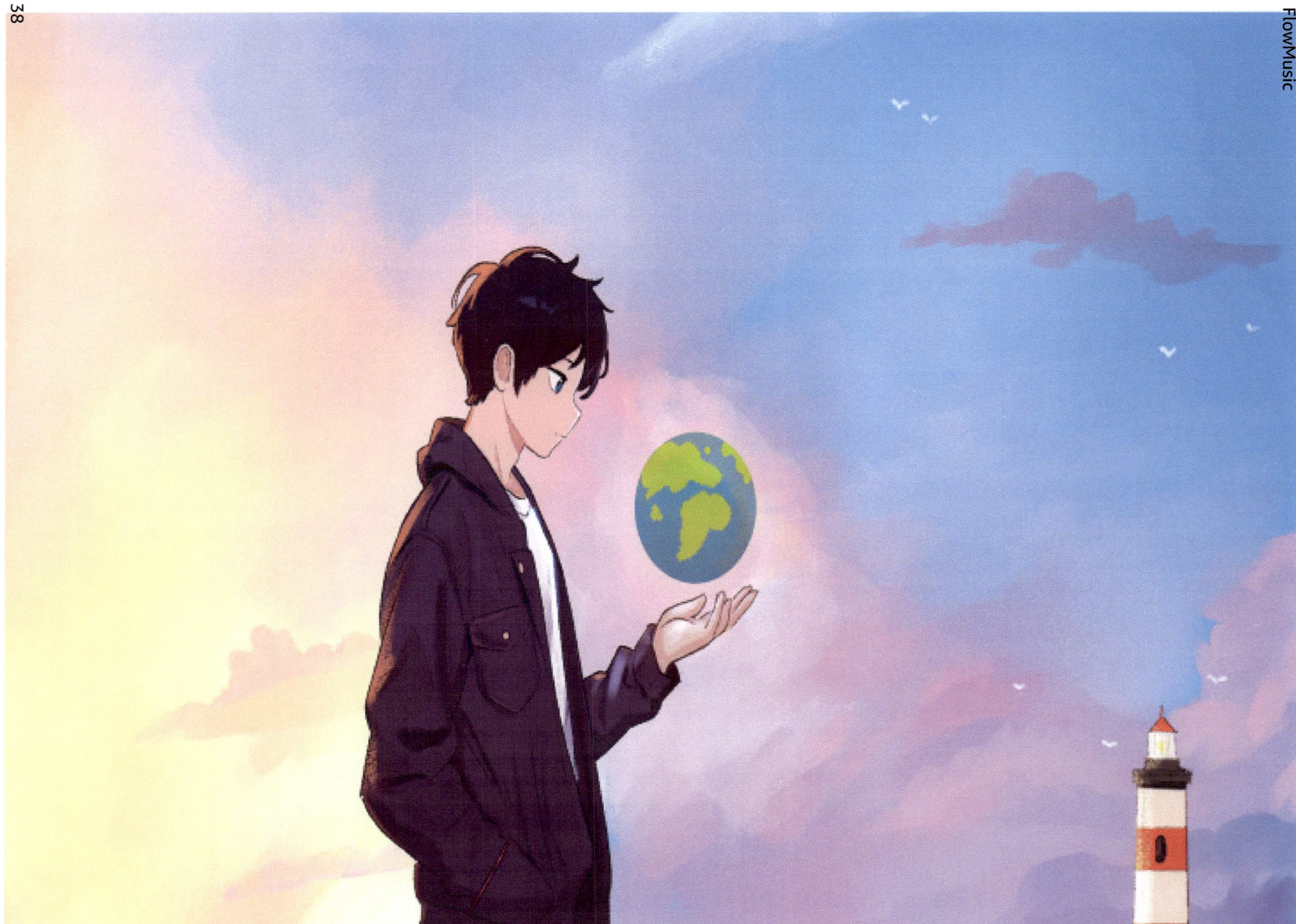

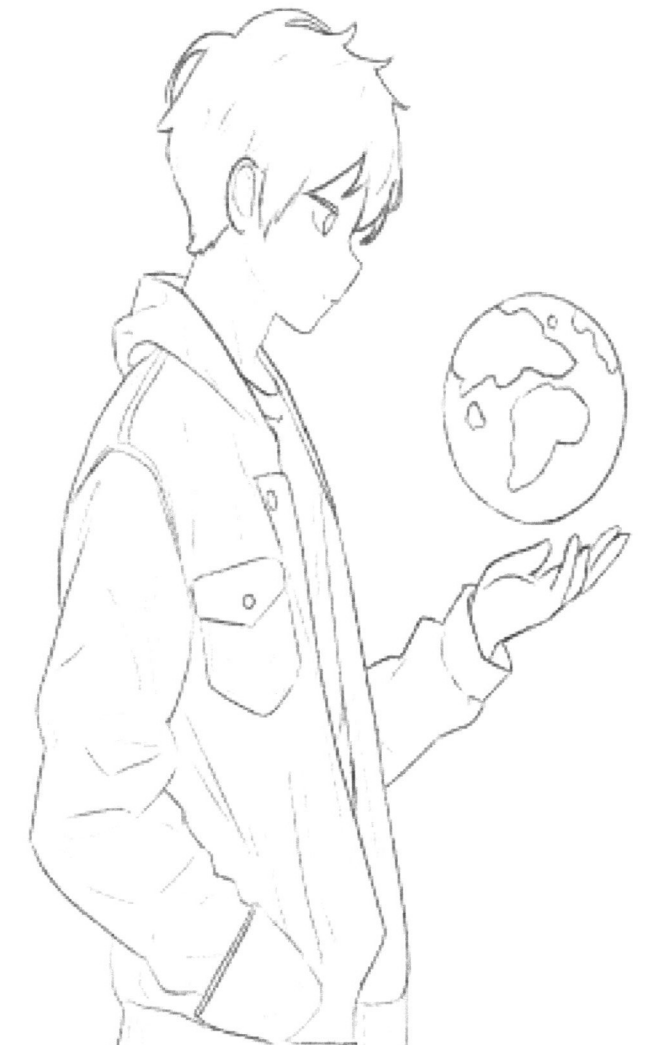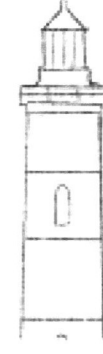

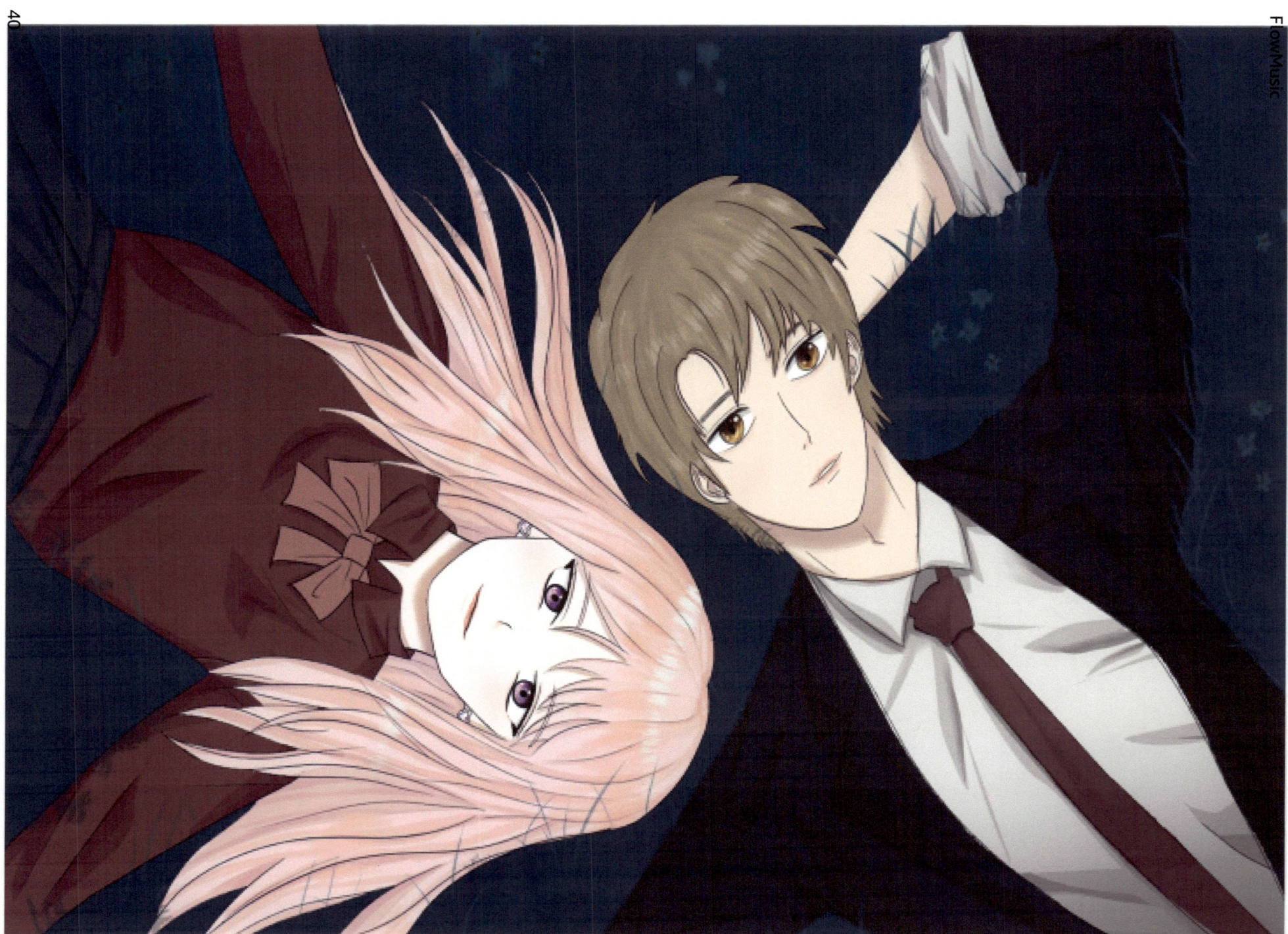

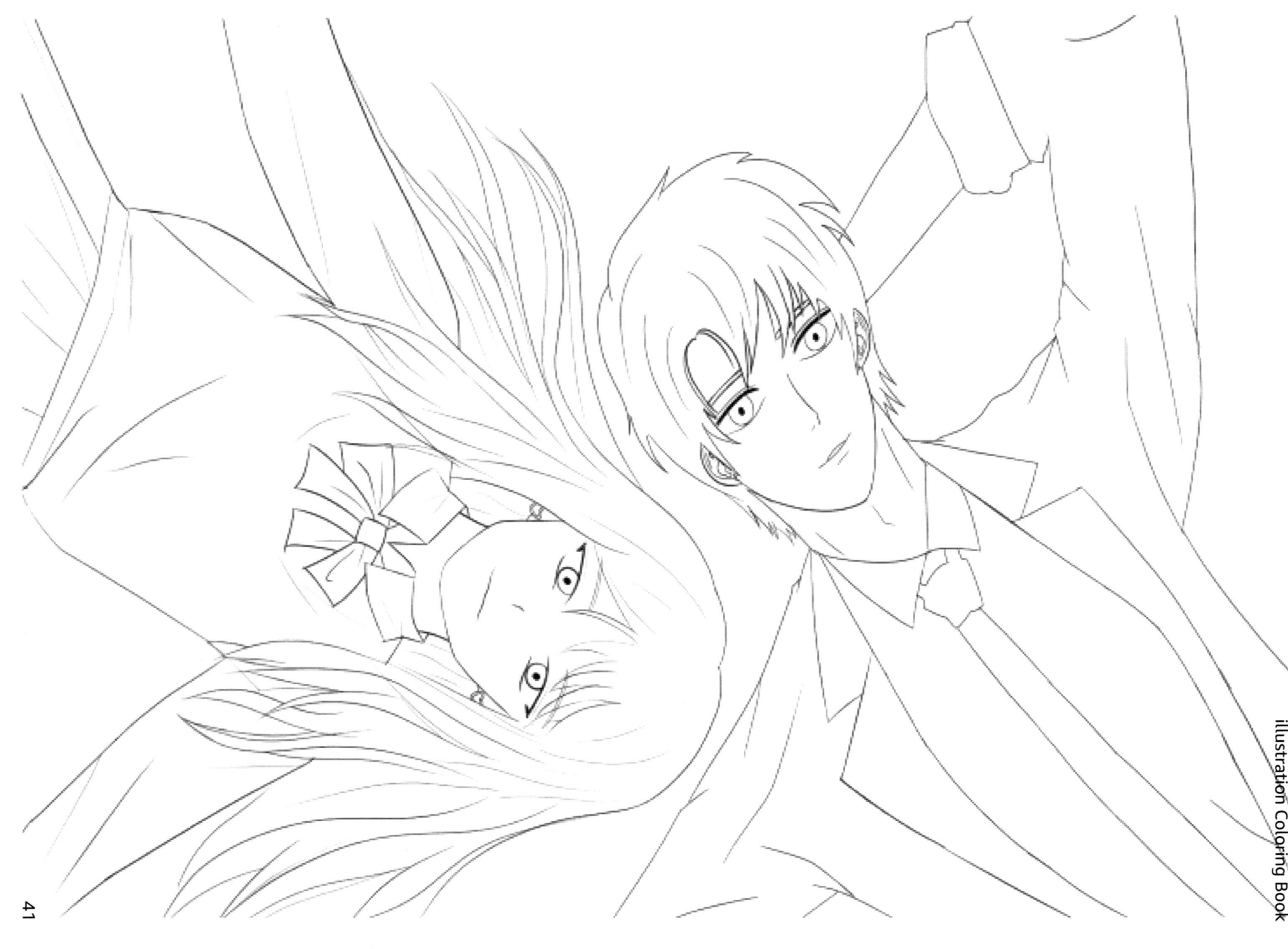

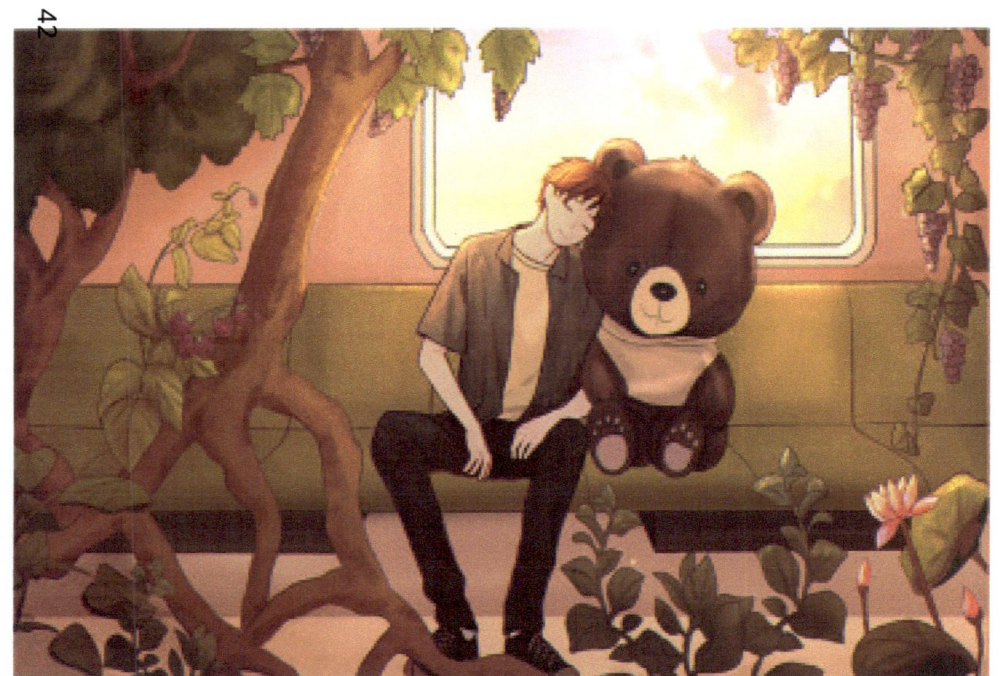
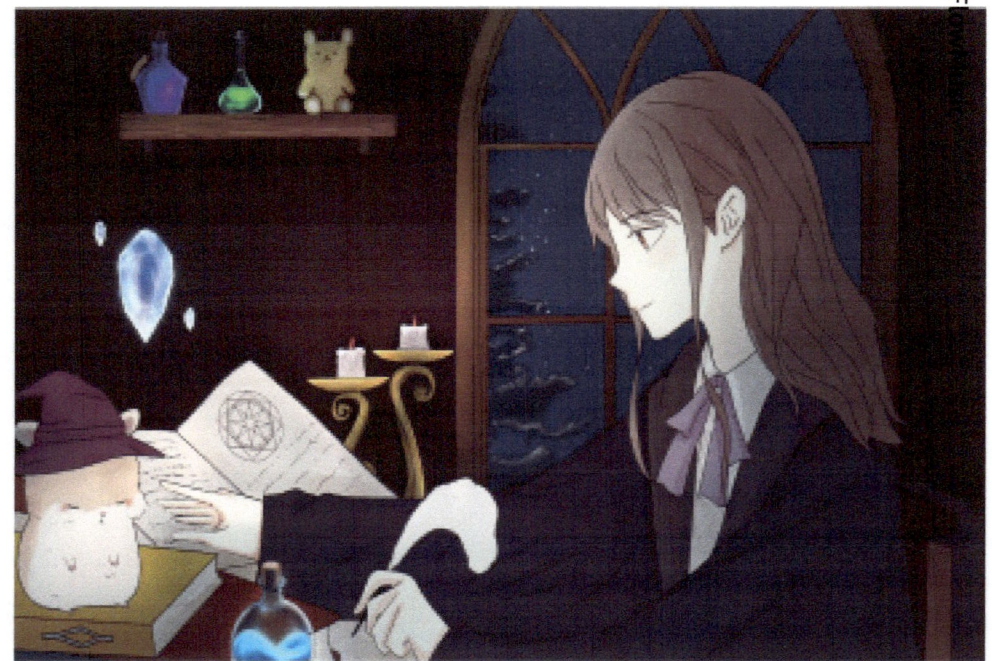
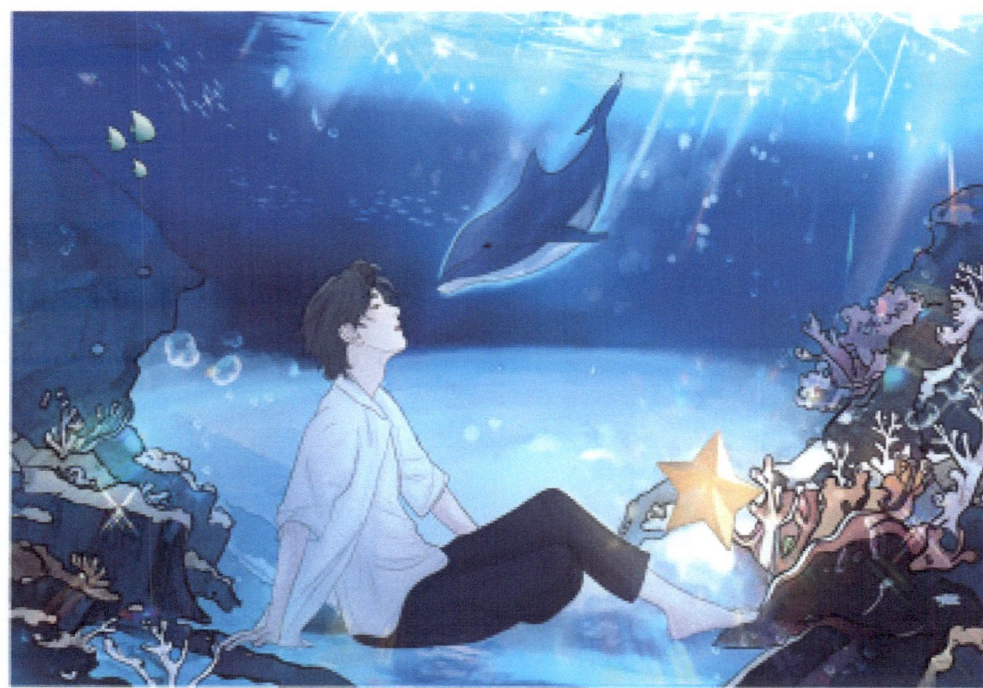
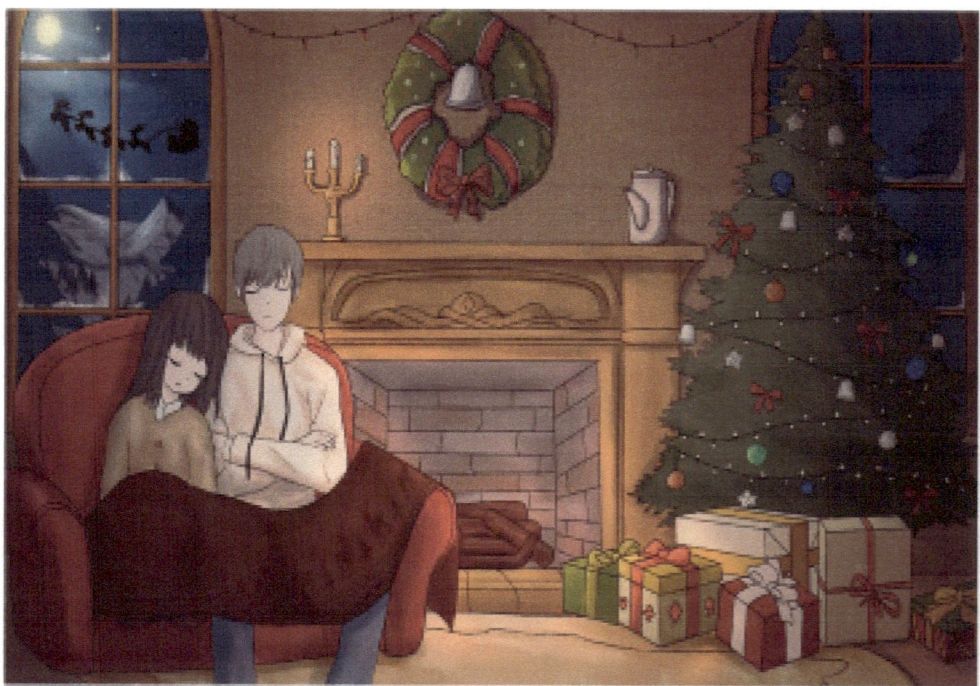

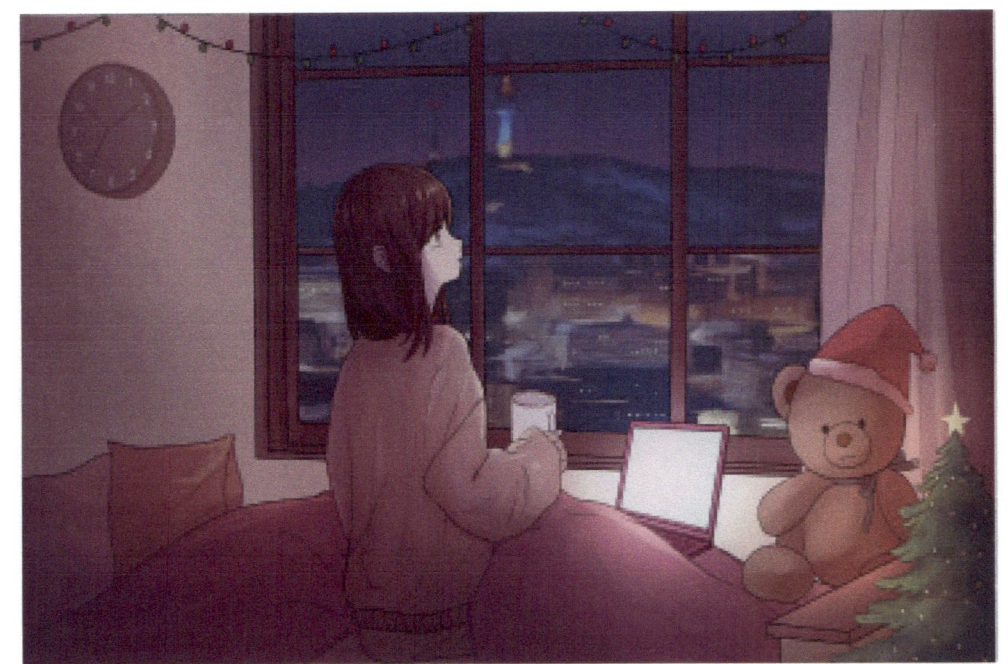
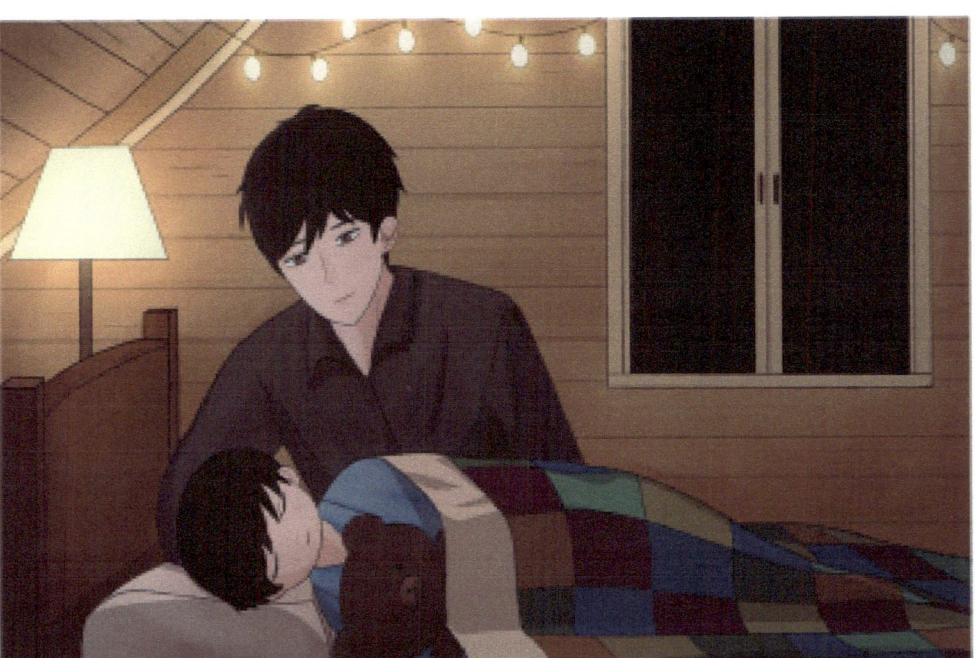
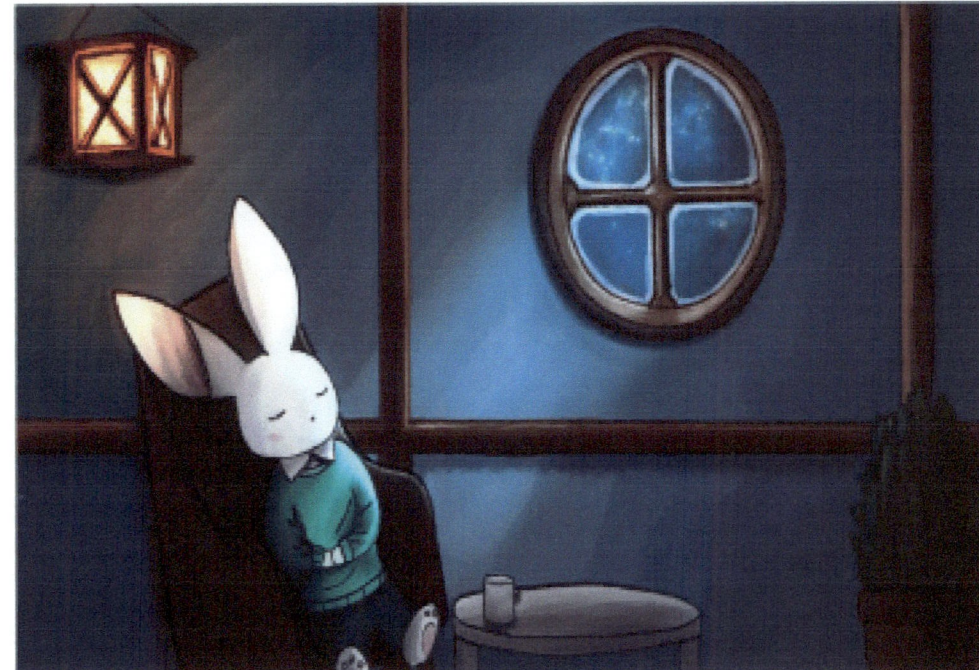
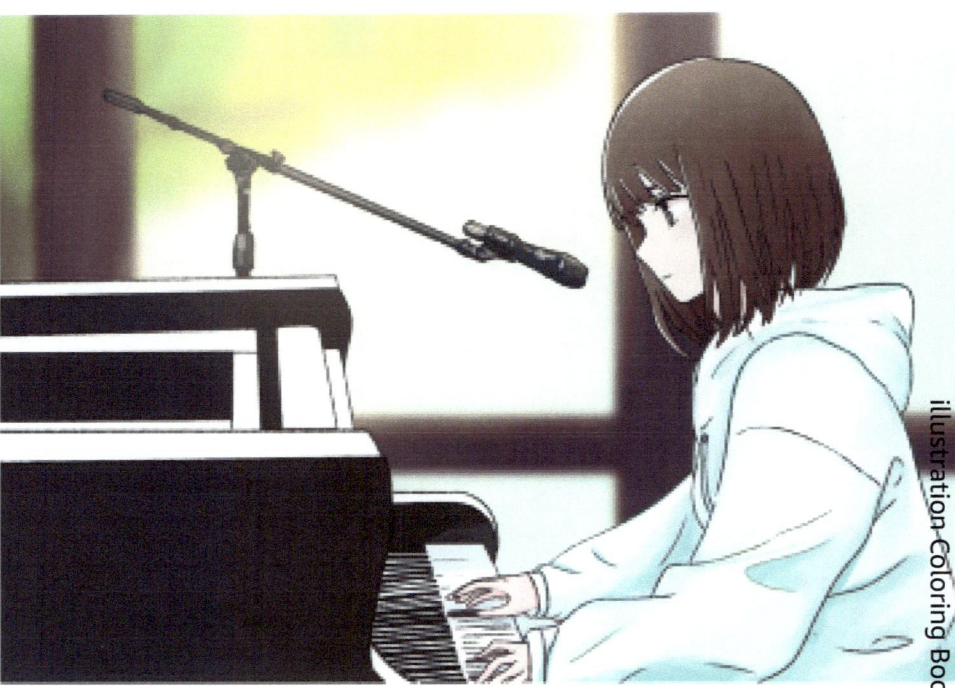

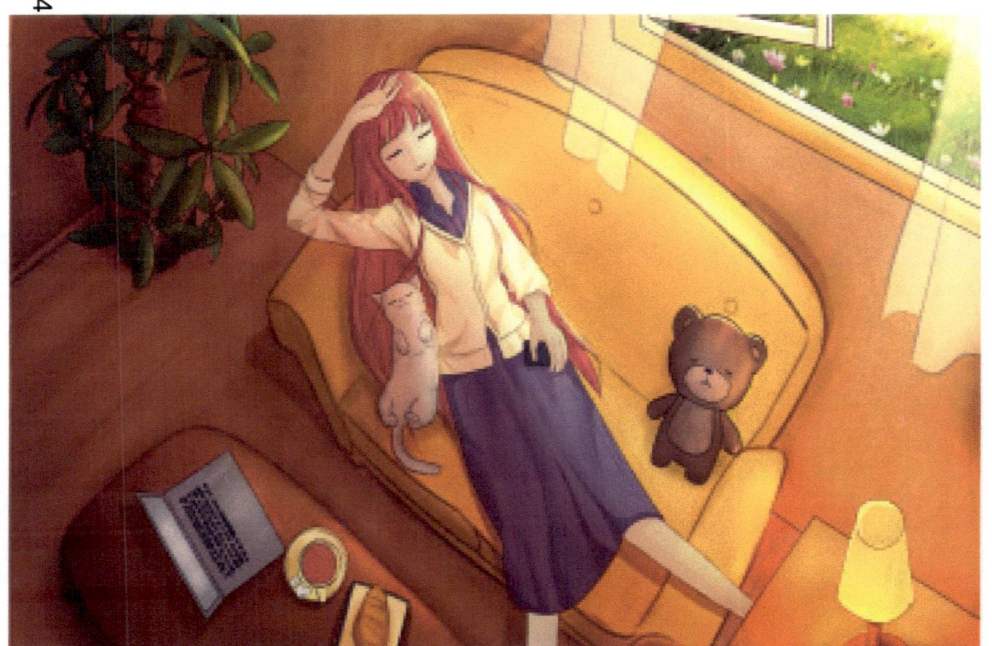
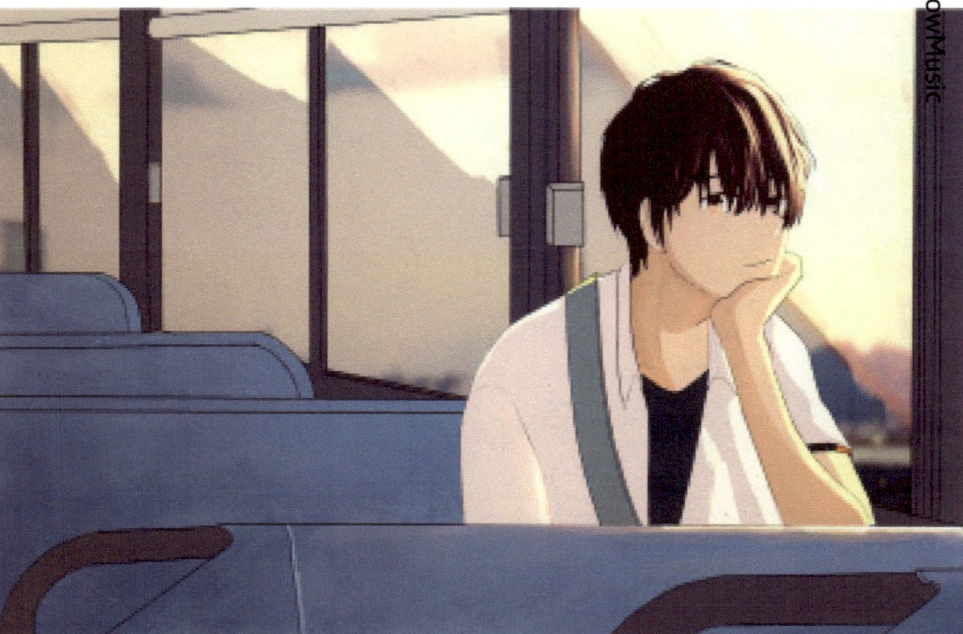
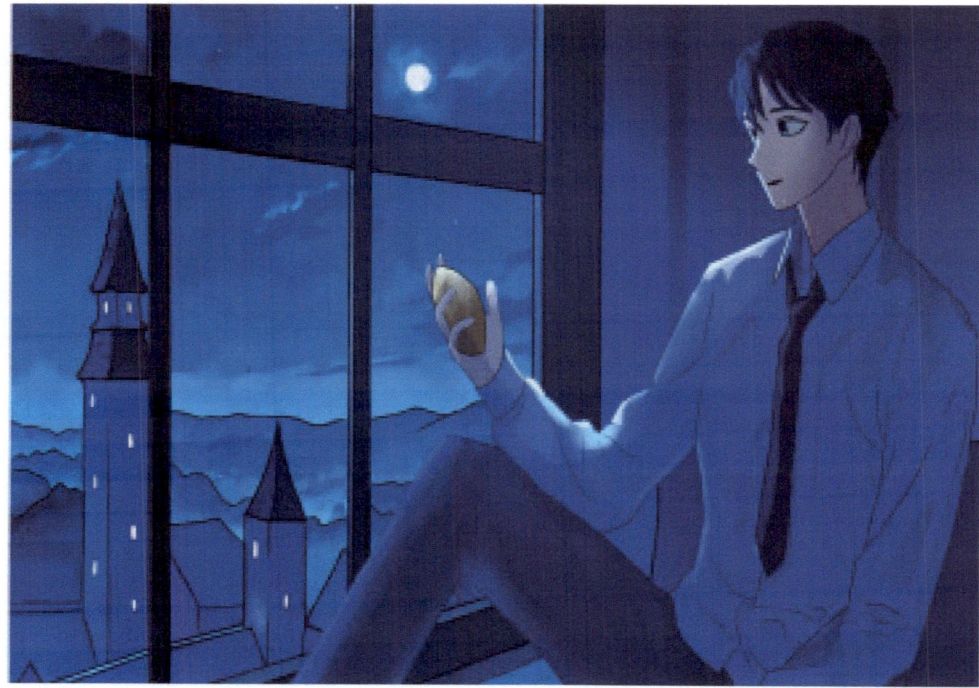
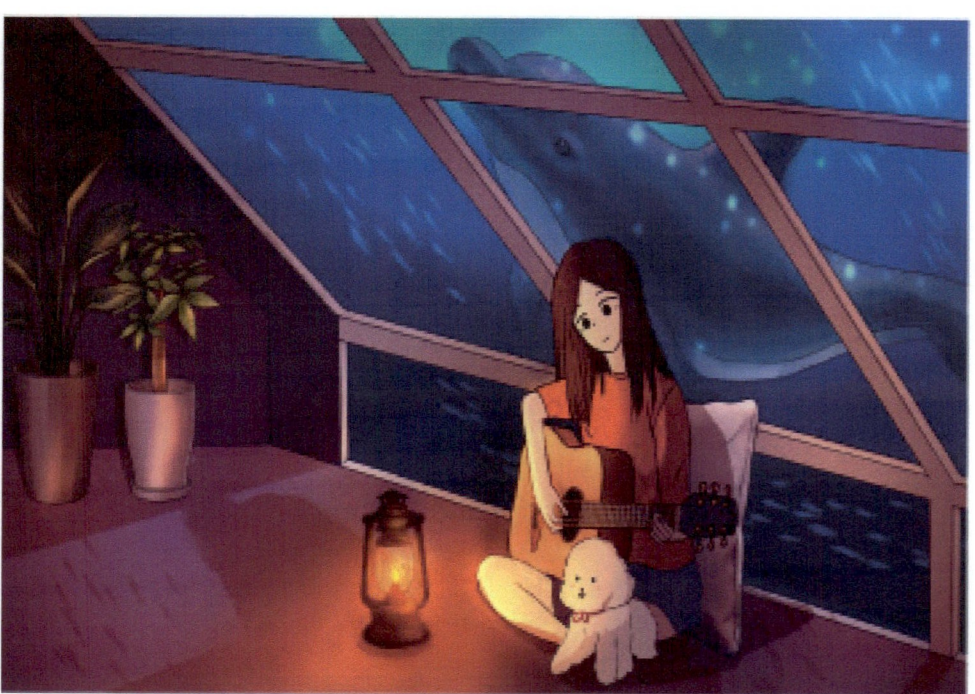

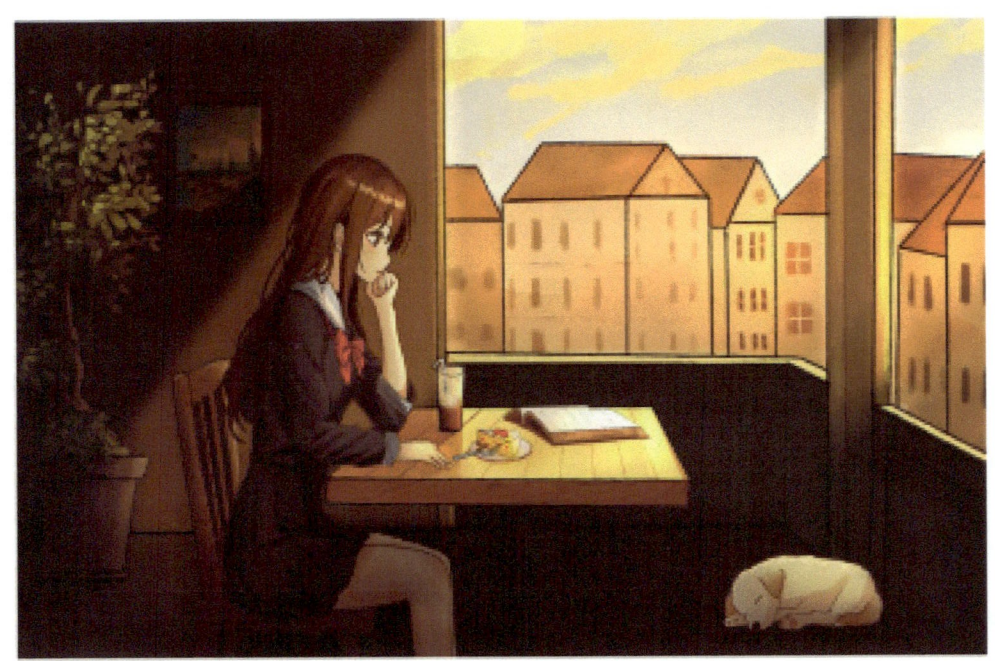
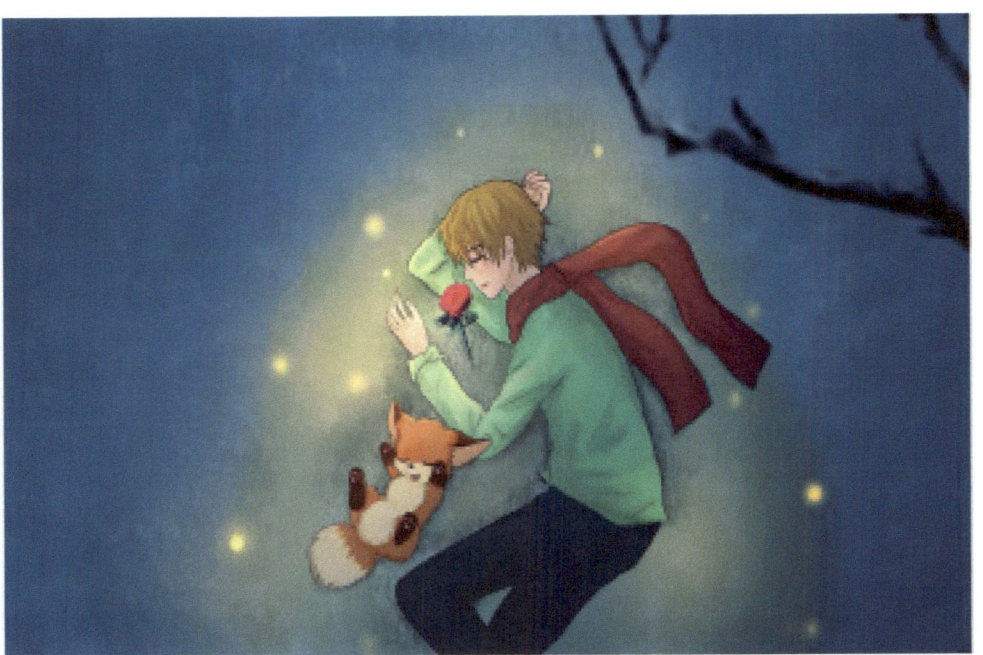
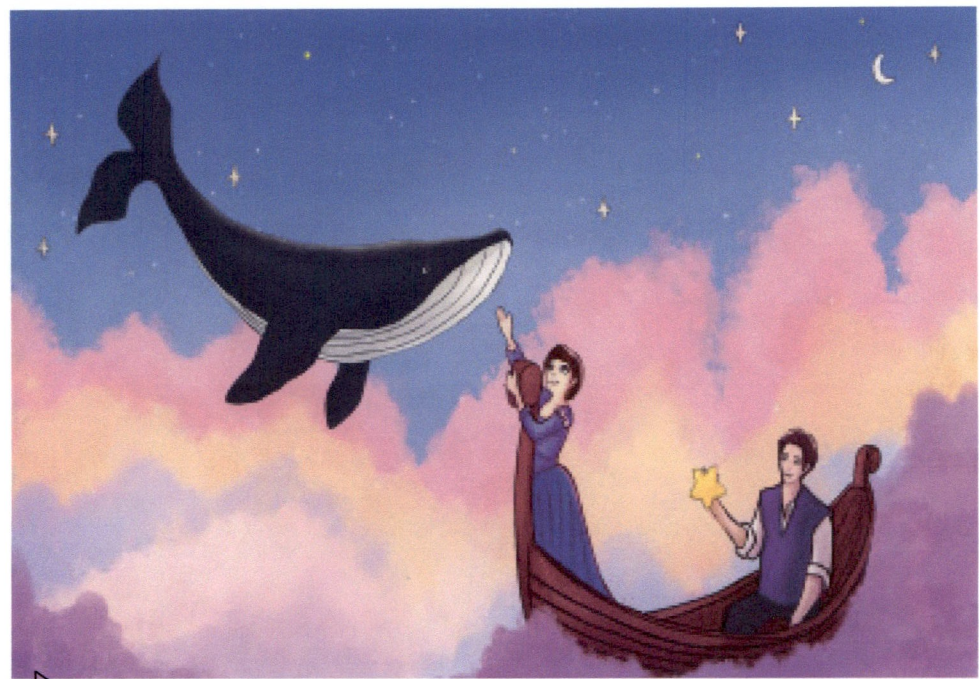
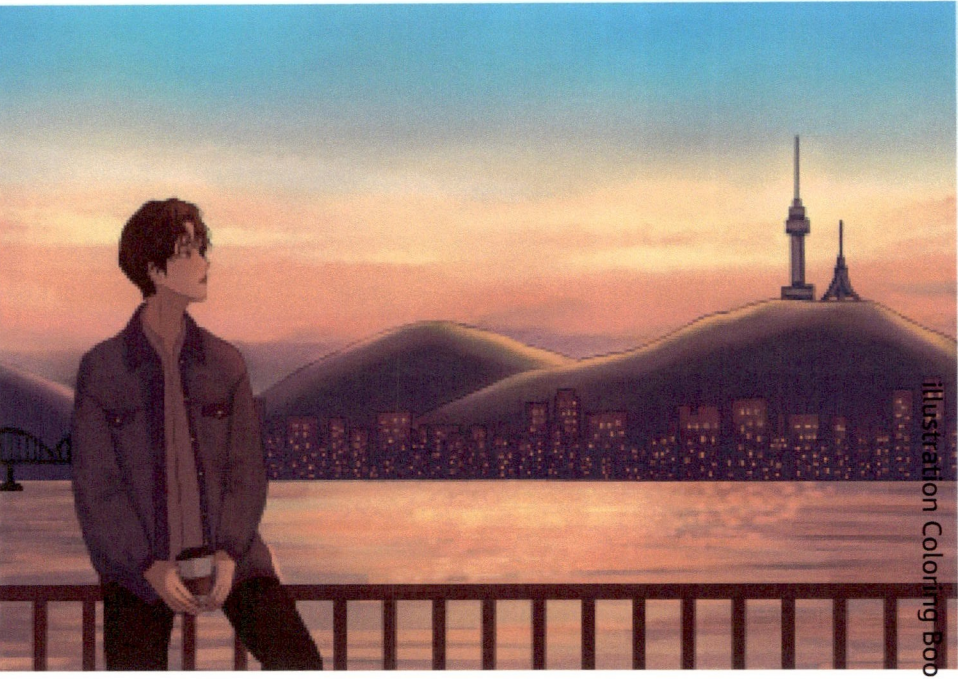

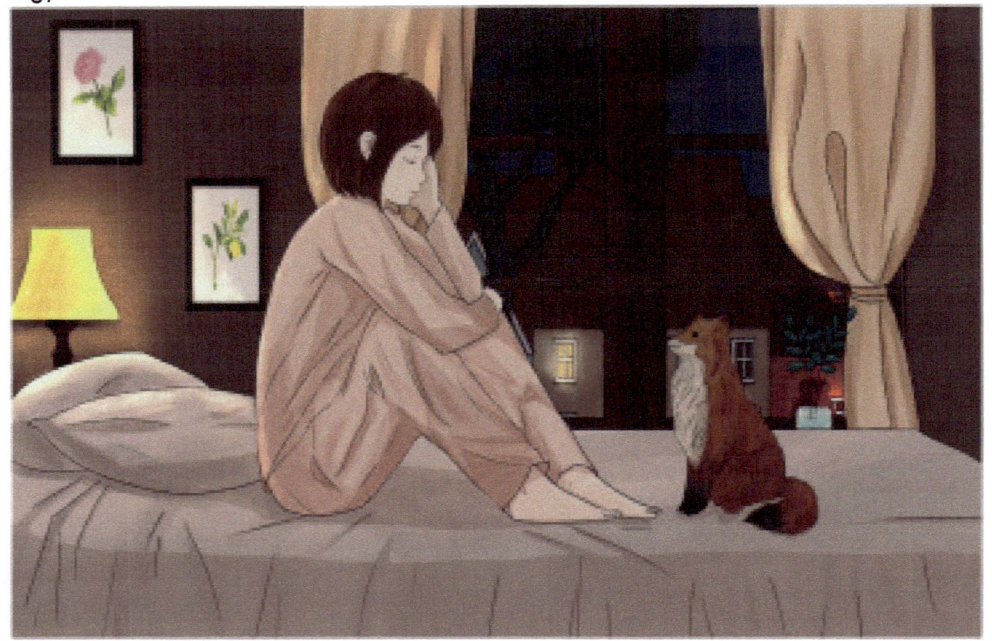
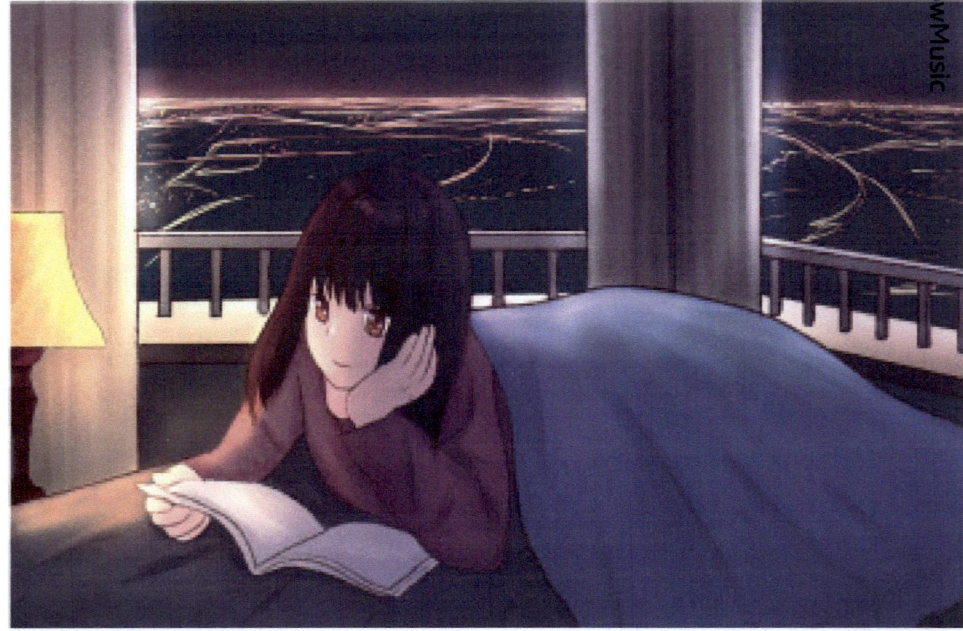
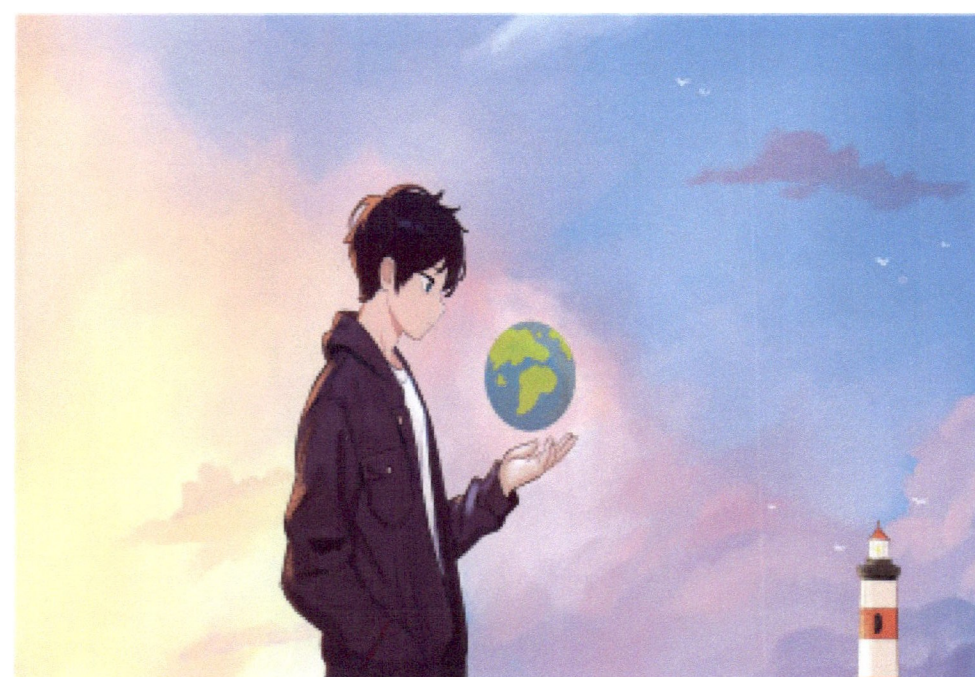
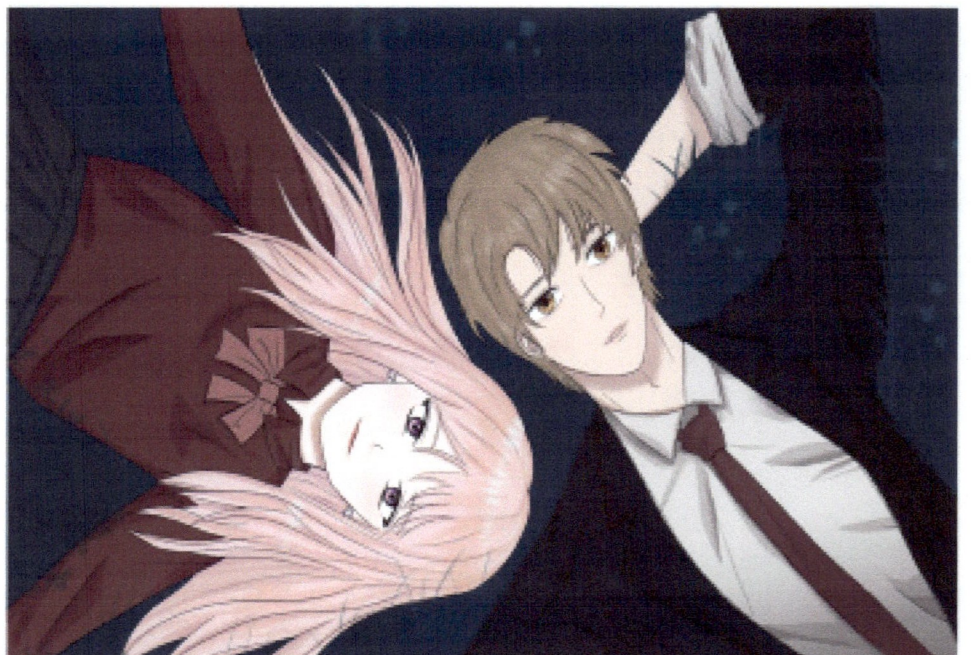

www.ingramcontent.com/pod-product-compliance
Lightning Source LLC
Chambersburg PA
CBHW040410220526
45473CB00004B/1191